You're not the only one on this Planet!

Observations on the absence of Civility: A Book of Leadership

By

Dr. John E. Mayer

authorHOUSE

1663 Liberty Drive, Suite 200
Bloomington, Indiana 47403
(800) 839-8640
www.authorhouse.com

First published by AuthorHouse 04/02/04

ISBN: 1-4184-2033-6 (e)
ISBN: 1-4184-2032-8 (sc)

Printed in the United States of America
Bloomington, Indiana

This book is printed on acid-free paper.

Table of Contents

Introduction vii

Chapter One Daily Life… 1

Opening Doors *1*

Walking *3*

Elevators *4*

Pet Owners *5*

Walking in Crowded Areas *8*

Space~~Body Boundaries *10*

Where we live *11*

Smokers *13*

Time *16*

Chapter Two In the Workplace… 18

Office Politics *18*

Chapter Three In Business… 23

Customer Service *23*

Attorneys *27*

The IRS *28*

Banks *29*

The Phone Company *31*

Insurance Companies *32*

Delivery Companies *35*

Doing our job *36*

The Myth of Technical Support *37*

Chapter Four At the Doctor's Office… **40**

  Waiting *40*

  Doctor's Attitude *41*

  Medical Staff *42*

  Receptionists *43*

  Patient Rights *44*

Chapter Five At the Health Club… **50**

  Cleaning up After Themselves *50*

  Care of Equipment *51*

  Loud, Obnoxious Behavior *52*

  Children at Health Clubs *53*

  Sporting Events *54*

  Public Restrooms *56*

Chapter Six Transportation… **58**

  Driving *58*

  Turn Signals *59*

  Tailgaters *60*

  Stop Signs *61*

  Littering *62*

  Turning *63*

  The Universal Sign of Friendship *64*

  Classic Driving Rudeness *64*

  Changing Lanes *65*

  Horns *66*

Pedestrians vs Vehicles 68
Handicap Spaces 69
General Courtesy 70
Driving and Sexism 71
Cars as Loudspeakers 71
Parking 72
Mobile Phones 74
Trucks 77
Air Travel—Passengers 79
Air Travel—Airline Personnel 82
Cyclists 83
Car Repairs 84
Hotels 86
Hotel Shuttles 87
Concierges 88
Hotel Amenities 89

Chapter Seven Conversation… **91**

Chapter Eight In Relationships… **98**
Listening 100
Defining 101
Relationship with Relatives 102
Immaturity 103
Dating 105
Voice Mail/Answering Machines 107

Privacy *108*

Chapter Nine In Sex **110**

   Selfishness in Sex *110*

   Loss of Sexual Interest *111*

   Machismo *112*

   Sex as a Tool *112*

   Sex and Attractiveness *113*

Chapter Ten In the Media **115**

Chapter Eleven In Restaurants **117**

   Loudness *118*

   Movie Theatres *119*

   Paying the Bill *119*

   Reception *120*

   Staff Attitudes *121*

Chapter Twelve At Home (Parenting and Family Relations) ... **123**

   Yelling *123*

   Setting Consequences *124*

   Kids and Drugs *127*

   Youth are COWs by Nature *129*

   Prevention Programs *130*

   Mental Health Professionals *132*

Chapter Thirteen *Turn in your own* COWs **135**

 **Introduction**

The United States of America is now and has been for some time the most powerful nation on earth. Unfortunately, great power does not automatically bestow upon a people refinement, consideration of others, or good manners. These are the qualities that define civil behavior, and how a society is defined as civilized by other nations and by history.

It has been observed by social scientists for some time that as the United States' power has increased, its civility has decreased. The mathematicians call this an inverse relationship. (Young readers please note, conjuring up terms like this is why you pay attention in high school algebra II. It DOES benefit you in the future.)

In the known history of the world the United States is not a unique example of this inverse relationship. The history of Western Civilization in particular is filled with examples of the powerful not being particularly cultured or benevolent toward both those they conquer and toward each other for that matter.

In fact, most often in history it has been the powerful conquerors who have been the most brutal toward each other and the people of the countries they have conquered. The Romans, the Huns, the Ottomans, the Vikings, Stalin's Russia, Hitler's Germany, the Iron Curtain, Sadaam's Iraq to name a few are all examples of brutes overpowering others and then ruling them without civility. The individual citizen had no value in these regimes. Instead, people were treated like objects.

The essence of the lack of civility is that a person treats another as though they have no value. The uncivilized person treats those around them as if they are less than human, no matter what that person's position in society, their race, or their religion.

Interestingly, in most cases these brutes' reign over the conquered peoples was short lived relative to the time line of Western Civilization. In contrast, the more civilized your culture the more longevity it enjoyed. The rulers in ancient Greece empowered conquered peoples by allowing them to govern themselves. The Greek conquerors often improved conditions by bringing the conquered peoples language, democracy, art, entertainment, property ownership and other advancements to the quality of life. They treated the people they governed civilly. Their reign over the Western world was long and prosperous. Their influence over the course of Western civilization is immeasurable.

Clearly history teaches us how to have a lasting reign. Brutish, uncivilized behavior gets you a short-lived and ugly control over other people, whereas, treat individuals with respect and civility and you will truly be the powerful master that will leave a long legacy on civilization.

This lesson can easily be applied to individual and small group behavior. As a supervisor, boss, even parent, rule over those subordinate to you in an uncivilized manner and you instantly lower performance of the actions you want. Taken a step further, simply treat those you are to lead with disrespect and you can guarantee that those under you will not perform to your satisfaction. The cornerstone of leadership is respect (civilized behavior) given to those you are entrusted to lead. As a consequence, this book is a handbook on how to be a better manager, parent or entrepreneur. To become successful in any of those roles one must incorporate civility into your social personality. It must become automatic behavior. Civility cannot just be turned on when one wants the result to benefit them. It should be practiced in our daily actions and repeated as we journey through the world. So this book represents a primer for developing excellent leadership skills that will benefit the reader in every walk of life.

So we have both history and successful managerial skills urgently calling out to us how we can become more powerful and lasting as a society and as individuals. But, we keep looking for power and success with short-term, instant gratification binoculars rather than a celestial telescope.

With the lens through which we look at our world we see that our way of life is a success. We often forget that the dominance of the United States is a recent phenomenon. Our status as the dominant society of this age emerged out of the devastation of World War II. This was only sixty years ago at the time this book is being written. Taking a lesson from the history of Western Civilization the length of the US reign as the most powerful nation on earth may depend more on how civil its citizenry is treated and how its citizens treat each other and not on its collection of bombs, planes and army men.

Again, make special note of this in your workplace, your family and in your community. Your reign depends less and less on your material things as it does on your civility to those whom you lead.

The purpose of this book is to raise the collective consciousness about civil treatment of one another in American society. It is also written to be a clarion call about where we are going as a society and as a world power.

More than ever in the history of the United States we are witnesses to the lack of civility in the citizenry of this country. At other times in our history as we were struggling to become a world power Americans went to great lengths courting the aspiration to acquire civility. But this quest has appeared to reach a sudden stop. Interestingly, it stopped around the time that we became the leading world power. It is as if the US no longer had to look over its shoulder toward other countries to gain a sense of culture. We made the fatal mistake of thinking that with power and status the nation would automatically gain civility. We stopped looking at our roots as a Western culture to grow civilly. We looked around and the US was the big dog in the pack. With the United States becoming the strongest world power other countries looked at the United States for world leadership and for the US's own brand of culture. But, again culture and civility are not the same.

Why did the United States drop our quest for civility once we became the dominant power? When the United States realized it was the most powerful nation on earth the insecurity about our origins ended. It appears that our need to act civil towards each other also ended about that time and the decline of civility is like a giant snowball rolling down a Colorado ski slope. Keeping in mind our history lessons, is this rolling snowball heralding the fall of this new empire?

This thundering snowball is being powered by the rampant plague of "I am the Center of the World" syndrome in the United States. For shorthand throughout the book I will hereafter identify this phenomenon by the acronym, COW (For Center Of the World.) and those afflicted with I am the Center of the World syndrome as COWs.

We did not create COWs overnight. The American personality has been characterized since the signing of the Declaration of Independence as self-reliant, egotistical and fiercely independent. The world views Americans through the lens of the Western cowboy. (Ironically, what was the occupation of the cowboys? Herding cows, of course! How apropos.) American culture fosters this image by honoring this example in American hero worship. Lindberg, Erhardt, DiMaggio, McArthur and Truman in real life, and John Wayne, Rocky, Rambo, Schwarzenegger and Monroe in myth all have been lionized by American culture and exported around the globe as the American ideal. The American public cannot get enough of the image of the loner facing adversity against all odds. But, not only have these real and manufactured legends helped to define the American culture, they have also shaped how we behave toward each other. These socially autistic characters have encouraged us to place a higher value on solitary survival rather than group success.

The tragedy of the COW syndrome is that it is ravaging our nation by sapping our power from within. Real power comes from having the security and confidence to be able to act civilly toward your fellow man. Power comes from giving and receiving respect from others not from imposing one's will on others, cheating others, taking advantage of others, physically beating others, and so forth. The great fear is that if we don't change course immediately and learn how to act civilly and value each and every citizen then we will fall prey to the fate of all historical brutes. If we can learn to act civilly we will not suffer inane laws, Presidents who look at us in the eye and lie, Watergates, Vietnams, etc.

This book will try to identify those common acts of uncivil, COW, behavior that sap our personal and collective power. The examples mentioned throughout this book are presented as highlights and not meant to be an exhaustive list. It is hoped by pointing out these occurrences in everyday life it will makes us more conscious of how poorly we treat each other.

Each person has dignity and value and we should behave toward them with no lesser standard. When appropriate the book will point out what we can do about our poor behavior toward each other so that we don't create more COWs and maybe even change those COWs already grazing in the lush bounty of this powerful country. The reader is alerted to these remedies throughout the book by a bulleted sub-title: <u>Tipping the COW</u>.

Because this book is only a start, in the final chapter are instructions on how you can submit your own observations and lessons on the lack of civility among us. Those observations that are unique will be added to the next volume of this book.

Enjoy, be aware, and don't become a COW.

Civility

Observations and Lessons

The situations mentioned in this book are not, nor are they intended to be representations of particular people, businesses, organizations or institutions in reality. The author intends no malice in presenting the examples offered in this book. The only intent here is to enlighten, entertain, inform, and to educate.

Chapter One
Daily Life…

Opening Doors

Count the number of people who say thanks while you open the door for them. Is it one in six? This occurs so seldom on the street that I often wonder if we have raised a whole generation of people who don't realize that all doors don't open automatically. That the other person with a hand on the doorframe is expending some effort to do that so that the door doesn't hit you right in your expressionless face. Or maybe these people don't even realize that there is a human being within their proximity? One could burn out a brain lobe ruminating on all the possibilities of why this COW behavior occurs.

<u>Tipping the COW:</u> (Remedies) Correcting this lack of civility presents some dilemma in and of itself. If while you hold this door open for the COW you sarcastically say, "Thank you" you are taking the chance that the COW will accept the thank you to mean, "Yes, you are the center of the world and thank you for brightening my dull insignificant life by passing through a door I am holding open for you. I have now touched greatness by being kind to that person who is at the center of the universe. Thank you again."

Another way to phrase this thank you is the following, "Not only will I hold the door open for you, but I will thank myself for you also. Thank you!" This may get the ungrateful COW to pay attention.

On the other hand the sarcastic thank you may just make the COW leave their narcissistic frame of reference and realize how uncivilized they are. So, giving that thank you provides at least a fifty-fifty chance of changing a COW. Do it.

I must confess that I cannot help but utter that 'thank you' to the COW as they pass expressionless past my effort. A real treat comes when the COW walks with a gait befitting their status as the center of the universe, slow and regal, and you can have the delight of letting the door slam on them after you realize you will not get any recognition for your initial act. I have done this on occasion and have most often found out that the COW keeps true to character and doesn't acknowledge my rudeness either. This is a demonstration of the fundamental characteristic of the COW syndrome, namely, these people <u>do</u> believe they are the only people on the planet.

Another of my favorite responses to holding a door for a COW is to pleasantly say, "Pardon me for holding this door for you, I didn't realize you have no manners." This phrase always seems to get a rise out of them.

At the very least, they acknowledge that there is someone else is walking on the planet.

Walking

COWs don't move their bodies from your path when your walking by a group of them. Well for that matter if you and an COW are walking straight at each other down a street, the COW will walk right into you unless you move. They're not playing 'chicken' with you, they just feel that they own the sidewalk. The amazing thing about this COW behavior is that they don't do this purposely. It is just that the COW is oblivious to others.

Watch them carefully next time you have to pass through a group of COWs to get to a doorway. Look into their faces, the COW doesn't blink an eye at your presence. They don't skip a beat in their conversation nor even exert the slightest glance in your direction. You could wave your hand back and forth in front of their face and they will simply stare ahead frozen into their life's agenda. It is truly an amazing phenomenon.

Tipping the COW: As COWs, maybe they will respond if you loudly ask, MOOOOOVE!

The important tip here is to say something, don't just let the COWs continue unabated with this boorish behavior. Try a phrase such as, '… pardon me I didn't realize this sidewalk was only for you'. Then, when they pass you still brandishing that self-absorbed stoic manner, mention something like this, 'my apologies again…you looked as though you spoke the language.'

Speaking of walking, an individual I know who is blind tells me that even though he is blind and swinging a red and white stick in front of him people still manage to plow into him regularly. Is there any rationale for this to happen in a civilized society?

Elevators

How about expecting another passenger to press the button for your floor in an elevator car for you when you have your hands full? Now this is a different type of situation than the one just described of walking down the street. By walking you are <u>active</u> standing in an elevator you are <u>passively</u> expecting a civil response. In this situation you are expecting someone else to take action for you because it is the civil thing to do.

<u>Tipping the COW:</u> Politely ask a fellow passenger, "Would you mind pressing my floor for me. I apologize my hands are full." Many people execute the first half of this remedy quite well. Adding the second half is an attempt to address the COWish behavior.

As of the writing of this book an elevator crashed to the basement of a building in Chicago because it was overcrowded. Eleven passengers were injured and one passenger was in critical condition. The elevator was just inspected one month before the accident. The fire department determined that the cause of the accident was due to overcrowding.

How many times have you seen that type of accident waiting to happen. An elevator door opens and the elevator is crowded, probably overcrowded, yet a COW waits on the floor that the door opens unto. That COW must jam their body into this already overcrowded elevator. Because that person is a COW they must squeeze themselves into this elevator and not wait for another one to arrive. After all, in the COW's belief system the elevator opened up just for them. Civil behavior would dictate that a considerate person seeing the elevator full would wait for the next elevator, but the COW's time is too valuable, more valuable than anyone else's on that elevator so they must press themselves into the overcrowded elevator at the expense of even the other passengers' safety.

Tipping the COW: Never do you hear another passenger speak up and announce to this COW not to enter this elevator. But, this is precisely what needs to be done in this situation. Let this COW know that there is no more room. Speak up, "The elevator is too crowded."

Here again we see social autism at work. Not only is the person entering the elevator a COW but also those on it are COWs as well. All are either unaware or ignorant of the danger of overloading the elevator or believes that the responsibility of managing the elevator belongs to someone else. COWs believe that every task on the planet comes with its own specialist for solving such problems. Thus COWs view themselves as being free from this social responsibility, thus socially autistic.

Pet Owners

Pet owners have a large number of COWs. The most obnoxious of their COW behavior is not disposing of dog waste. One of the most heinous offenders is a fellow in Chicago who carries paper toweling in his hand while he walks his dog only to never use it for the apparent purpose. He even stoops over as if he is going to pick up the waste only to straighten up and not touch his dog's golden droppings. The city of Chicago recently began to enforce ordinances that carry heavy fines if dog owners don't pick up after their dogs. (Here, Here Chicago!) Apparently, he carries the paper towels just in case a police officer is nearby so he won't get a fine for not cleaning up after the dog.

Come on, why go to the length of carrying the toweling and not bending down picking up the waste, carrying it a few feet and disposing of it in a garbage can? Would you take toilet paper off the roll wave it around your nose and then not use it?

Recently, a friend of mine related to me that she has seen another guy carry one of these shovel-like disposal apparatuses, bend over and approach his dog's waste only to leave it ferment there until it finds a home on the sole of someone's shoe.

Is there some fraternal men's organization that teaches these guys such imbecilic behavior. There couldn't have been two of these fellows, but in fact there are. Do they belong to a gentleman's (sic) club that starts every meeting with a pledge that they shall not under any circumstances stoop so low in life to dispose of any waste? Are their toilets at home totally clogged with their own waste less they violate the credo of their organization? *Thou shall not flush toilets, as they are beneath us.* Come on, what could possibly be the motivation behind this behavior?

But these guys are just amateurs compared to the president of the condo association at an exclusive and famous Chicago high rise. This woman owns two medium sized dogs and out of sheer laziness and lack of concern for others, she allows them to urinate and defecate in the carpeted public hallway of the building by ushering them just outside her door when it is the dog's time to relieve themselves. Sadly, what is most notable about her is not the crude behavior, but the fact that she is the president of the condo association. Remarkable as this woman's behavior is, other luxury high rises have similar crude inhabitants. Some have had to fence off sections of stairwells because tenants use them as bathrooms for their dogs. These same stairwells are littered with countless cigarette butts and old chewing gum. If people don't take concern over where they live they probably won't take concern over where you and I live. These people violate the very essence of the definition of civility.

Some COWs may have been created by people becoming desensitized by continual exposure to such conditions. When COWs contribute their gum, cigarette butts and doggy doughnuts to the environment, they also contribute to the desensitizing that creates more COWs. Someone else will clean up after me, whether it is the gum getters, butt brigade, or the poop patrol. They don't realize that it is their responsibility to do these acts. Owning a dog is a responsibility and to find out whose responsibility just follow the leash upwards.

Tipping the COW: Don't be afraid to speak up against these COWs. If you don't you deserve the dog dung on your shoe. Another tip that is polite yet effective is to ask dog walkers if they have a bag. If they do, responsible dog walkers appreciate being asked and are proud of the fact that they are carrying a bag. If they don't, BAM! Now you can lay into them and shame them for their COWish behavior. Maybe you could even follow them to their house and scrape the dog dodo on <u>their</u> door mat to even the score of the countless number of times you have had to do this at your front door.

Dog owners can be particularly savvy with this last tip by always carrying extra bags with them when you walk your dog. When you encounter one of these COWs and you ask if they have a bag and you receive the COWish brain dead response, reach in your pocket, pull out your extra one and wait to watch them do the deed. Wouldn't it be great fun to watch this COW do something that obviously is against their grain?

Walking in Crowded Areas

One would think that walking down the street is an as innocuous activity as drinking a glass of warm milk, but yes, rude COW behavior can engulf it as much as any. A favorite example is from a woman that works in a crowded downtown area. One evening she was walking to the train station along with the shuffling hordes of nine-to-five workers that populate this large metropolis. The stream of walkers flow with a current that is unbreakable. If you have never experienced this push of humanity it is a unique experience. On one evening as this woman was navigating the current of bodies like so many past evenings, she went to make her usual turn at the corner where her particular train departed and as she turned a woman either turned into her or she turned into the woman. Regardless, of who was at fault, the stranger fell to the pavement and caught her fall with her hand. Even though she was without physical injury, the woman and her husband who was walking with her lashed out with a barrage of foul language, accusations, and demands. It turns out that the woman and her husband were attorneys walking home from their offices. They demanded to examine the driver's license of the woman who was both profusely apologetic and intimidated. The husband and wife lawyers cried lawsuit and indeed did file not only aggravated battery charges against the walker, but filed a civil suit as well. The woman was frightened and emotionally distraught for months. All over bumping into someone walking down the street.

Our empathy for each other has deteriorated so much that the simple act of walking down the street and tripping has now become an explosive confrontation that potentially may cause ruin to this working woman. She may lose her job if her criminal charge holds up in court and all the legal fees will certainly financially ruin her that she will have to pay to fight both the criminal and civil lawsuits. Because she is a nervous person by nature and easily intimidated all the while she will emotionally suffer as this is all being inflicted upon her.

Tipping the COW: Try not to follow the frenetic cattle herding to the train. Don't let the herding mentality suck you in. Go slow, take your time and go the road less traveled.

But, if you do find yourself accidentally bumping into a lawyer on the street here's a tip. Make a couple of calls to other lawyers in your community. You'll find that it won't take you many calls to find one who doesn't like the one you bumped. Lawyers with this COW personality seem to make enemies readily. You'll find that you just may have your pick of

9

attorneys who will represent you on this frivolous matter and be hyper-aggressive on the case to boot.

Space~~Body Boundaries

COWs do not respect others' body space. Why should they? They act toward others as if they are not even there. So, you will find COWs standing in front of your way, taking your place , cutting in line at events, complaining about waiting, pushing, shoving and other COW like behavior.

Traditionally, in Western society respecting the space of another is a mark of the polite and courteous. It is part of our culture, our civility. In contrast, many other societies do not treat body boundaries and space in the same regard. For example, in Japanese society space, privacy and body boundaries are handled almost completely the opposite of how American's sensibilities are in regard to these behaviors.

You can best observe these differences on the beach in Honolulu, Hawaii because this tourist spot is popular with both American tourists with Japanese tourists. Americans painstakingly hunt for a spot on the beach where no one else has laid claim for that patch of sand. Japanese sunbathers, on the other hand, will routinely set their blankets as close to the next person's as possible. You will see this even when the beach is mostly empty. This is not done consciously nor is it done because they seek out the closeness of others. It is a cultural dynamic that relates to an entirely different concept of space and body boundaries.

It is our cultural norms that dictate how civil behavior toward others will be acted out. In the United States civil behavior dictates that one person respects the space of the other. Only COWs do not respect the space of others. They are by definition abnormal.

Tipping the COW: Let COWs know you're there since they surely don't realize you are in the same space they are occupying. A simple statement such as, "I'm in here too," is sufficient to let the COW know you don't accept their ignorance. The main goal is to let the COW know that you are offended by their ignorance.

Quite often we are overly polite toward COWs rude behavior and space is a great example. We move and let the COW take our space. We sit in silence while the COW cuts in line. We alter our behavior when the COW sits down on top of our beach towel. From now on ask the COW to move. (Or moooooooove.)

Why do COWs have bells? Because their horns don't work. Does your horn work? Then alert a COW.

Where we live

How much longer do we have to put up with and indulge the whining of those people who have chosen to live right next to an airport, sports stadium, amusement park or other such large public venue and then they complain and lobby the local government to take care of their noise and nuisance issues. In the Chicagoland area there are two extreme examples of this COW-like behavior, Wrigley Field and O'Hare Airport.

The baseball park Wrigley Field sits squarely in a residential neighborhood. Several decades ago prior to Wrigley Field being discovered as a quaint picturesque place to watch a baseball contest (If one can use that term given the play of the Cubs.) the neighborhood around Wrigley Field was run down and property values were low. Suddenly Wrigley Field becomes popular with a new generation and it becomes a hot place to be in Chicago. Bars and other service establishments sprung up like wild fire. The property values of the surrounding houses also sprung up with the resurgence of the neighborhood. Now, dozens of public interest groups have been formed to "protect" the neighborhood from the throngs of fans who stampede through this residential area. These groups are vehement about lobbying the city government to control noise, litter, drinking, rowdiness, parking and a number of other acts that come with going to the ballpark. These groups are calling for millions of public funds to be spent to "protect" their neighborhood. Yet the Wrigley Field 'neighbors' erect their own stands on top of their roofs and charge money to private parties during games. Come on, by definition, without Wrigley Field there would be no Wrigleyville neighborhood. COWs stop your mooooing.

Tipping the COW: These people knew full well what they were buying into when they purchased a house in this community and their property values have raised considerably by being near Wrigley Field, airports, and other such places. Now they want the other citizens in other areas of the city to open their pockets to increase their property values even more. Shut up and enjoy you profits!

Smokers

Sure we all feel sadness toward those people who have an addiction that is slowly killing them, but we could conger up more empathy for them if smokers respected the rest of us a bit more.

The most obvious offense the smokers inflict upon the rest of us is that they stink. No matter what they do or how they smoke, they smell differently than the rest of us. And, because less and less people are smoking the smell of the smoker stands out all the more. Ever go to the house of a smoker and visit for a while. After you get back to your house, you'll notice that the clothes you wore reek from cigarette smoke. There is no way to get that odor out but to wash those clothes thoroughly. You can open windows while you visit all you want and your friend can even cut down on the number of cigarettes they would normally smoke but you will still reek from cigarette smoke. You hair will smell and your skin will smell like cigarettes.

Tipping the Cow: Never wear your favorite clothes to a smoker's house. That's unfortunate if the person is someone you want to impress, but save the clothes from your 'A' rack for the times when they are visiting you or when you go out somewhere in public together.

Another good tip about visiting a smoker's house is to leave your coat, sweater, blazer, etc. outside in the hall closet, or the foyer, or even outside of their door. In this way your coat will not get the door prize of your friend's smoke odor. It's important to save your coats from the invasion of smoker's smell because it's harder to clean your coats as often and it's definitely more expensive to keep cleaning them. Can you imagine taking your leather coat over to a smoker's house and draping it over the sofa while you visit? That lovely evening of pleasant conversation and maybe a few drinks will cost you $50, the average cost of cleaning a leather coat.

Smell is the most noticeable of the offenses smokers force us to endure, but another crude habit of smokers is that they are constantly trying to bend the non-smoking regulations. Like bandits on the run, they sneak into hallways, closets, they turn on kitchen exhaust systems to cover up their secret, and they do almost everything and anything to make smoking convenient for them and offensive to us. So what happens? We constantly encounter smokers in their secret cocoons in the most unlikely and unexpected places. Non-smokers are startled by opening doorways only to find an addicted smoker huddled just inside the door, their cheeks inverted as they suck on their white paper filled with tobacco.

Hidden nooks are not the only spaces that smokers are making their private liars for indulging their addiction. The outside of every office building today has a cabal of smokers huddling around the front doors and these smokers often block the entrance to others trying to egress. This is particularly true in cold or rainy weather. During bad weather, the smokers cluster around the doorway's warmth like varmints clawing for shelter.

Tipping the COW: Municipalities should enact laws that forbid these gangs of addicted smokers to loiter. These smokers and their companions seduce even non-smokers into their threatening catatonic stances outside of doorways. Standing stationary and hunched over, the only movement of their body is their forearm repetitively bringing the addictive leaves into their lips. These sick individuals who must obsessively indulge their addiction at any cost cast a threatening presence on the entranceways across America. It is time to clean up the façade of our buildings.

Smokers also are huge litterers. This is another COW behavior of smokers. Smokers seem to feel that the remains of their cigarettes are invisible so they throw them aimlessly into the street. They throw them as they walk, they throw them out of their cars, and they throw them out of open house windows. Cigarette butts fill our streets and make our communities appear as though the residents are animals. If not animals, it certainly makes communities appear as if they don't care.

Why do smokers throw the away the focus of their addiction when they are finished? Are they ashamed? Are they in denial. No, they must truly feel that their cigarettes are invisible so the remains of their cigarettes will lie unnoticed resting in peace. Maybe that is why this addiction proliferates, those addicted feel that their smoking is invisible. They don't see themselves hunched over, cheeks sucking in like victims of the plaque. They don't see themselves standing outside of buildings like outcasts, put out into the streets like thieves. And they certainly don't see themselves gasping for their last breath.

Tipping the COW: Smokers need to look at themselves. Let's make it our responsibility to point out their behavior to them. If a smoker throws a cigarette out of their car window and if your have the chance, at the next stop light ask them, "Didn't you have enough money for the ashtray?" or "Next time you buy a car, spend a little more and pony up for an ashtray."

Smokers should take a good long look at themselves. It is their free will whether they want to smoke or not, but please smokers take a look what you inflict upon the rest of us. Don't be a smoking COW.

Time

What's the deal with Daylight Savings Time? Do we need it? Does it serve any purpose? Does it make our lives any easier? We once were are largely agricultural society. I believe that was prior to the industrial revolution. This change in our work force occurred in the mid to late 1800's. yet we are clinging on to a custom that made sense only in the lives of works in the 1800's. Can anyone explain why or what is the value of this custom?

Tipping the Cow: Why don't we, you and I, just decide not to follow this cute, antiquated social custom any longer? Indiana and some other parts of the country don't, so why can't anyone just decide to be just as stubborn? Be your own person, pick you favorite time of year, either the dainty, 'Fall Back' or the whimsical, 'Spring Ahead', and set your watch to that time and start to live your life by that clock. Oh, your boss will get mad at you? Simply tell him that you don't follow outdated social customs any longer. Explain how this is a '1st Amendment' issue. You have the right to follow whatever social customs you desire in a free country, just like freedom of religion.

In fact encourage all your friends and family to join us with our new time perspective. This could even grow into that great American pastime of creating a 'movement' or cult around a behavior like this. We'll have our own cult of Americans that don't believe and won't follow Daylight Savings Time. Now we have something here.

Chapter Two
In the Workplace…

Office Politics

The high temple of uncivilized, COW, behavior is modern office politics. People maneuver themselves in the workplace with a constant mindset of CYA (Cover Your Ass). Instead of the focus being on how well one does their job, people work with a paranoia about how they are going to look or be held accountable for their actions. One certainly doesn't find accountability and craftsmanship in the workplace any longer. Evidence the fact that you do not see plaques or pretty posters in those ubiquitous motivational mall stores that announce, 'Give your best to others' or 'Make your work art'. Instead most of the messages at these places read some variation of be quiet and don't make waves or escape and find inner peace. Industry doesn't value the worker that takes responsibility, has the customer's satisfaction in mind and takes pride in their work.

A fellow I know worked in a large bank in the mortgage lending department. He was a dinosaur. He had been doing mortgages for forty years. Recently he was laid off from the job he held at the same bank for all those years. He was too slow for the modern pace of business. He did his initial paperwork by hand. A painstaking process but extremely accurate. In fact, in this computer age it is an accepted practice at the large banks that mortgage papers will be sent back many times internally and then again many more times between the direct lenders and the clients before a loan is consummated. This 'bounce-back' expectation is built into the banks auditing system. Errors are corrected, options are added that were not thought of, and a multitude of basic mistakes have to be corrected. With my friend's documents this did not occur. He prided himself on his record that not a single document was returned after he sent it onward for approval. Further, he saved an entire file drawer of thank you letters and notes from clients for whom he saved thousands of dollars by discovering unrecorded interest payments, overcharges, and other oversights that only a human pro would have an intuitive feel for. Of course, his meticulous work couldn't fit into the marketing push of "Rapid Returns". You can't give a fast food mortgage when you're doing it by hand. He was let go in favor of the mistake filled, ping-pong like work habits of the technology dependent worker who pushes the papers along more rapidly only to have them ping pong back and forth until correct. You get fast answers, but fast quality. Rejected loans that could have been made and accepted loans full of mistakes. His demise was also sealed by correcting the mistakes of his immediate supervisor who didn't welcome the potential of having their inadequacies highlighted in the Cover My Ass environment of the modern workplace. In his late fifties when this occurred, he has little chance of finding another job in the industry he knows so well and has mastered. The boss is a COW.

Tipping the COW: Why isn't there a place for a worker who is such a specialist? Let him handle jumbo loans from large important customers. They expect this type of personal service.

The American business has become so socially autistic that they no longer seek to serve the public but serve themselves through the public. Who do you talk to when your mortgage does not go through? Why, you need to talk to 'so and so' and so and so says, 'no, you need to talk to that other person' who in turn directs you to yet another specialist. Because responsibility can be passed from one person to the next, the company is left without a moral conscious. It has no soul.

Your credit was not approved? It's no longer the bank's or lender's fault, but it is the fault of the score you received from an outside credit report agency. Ask the credit report agency why and you get a letter that says it also isn't their fault either as they just advise the lender/bank. Doesn't this ping pong game of responsibility sound all too familiar? It should, this is the same, "I'm just following orders" excuse given by the Nazi SS troopers in WWII.

Other workplace behavior is just as crude. Take the example of management that makes decisions without any input from those actually doing the work. Someone I know drives a truck and delivers fresh food. He drives a medium-sized panel truck. It is ten years old yet has been reliable and has a low service record. Corporate headquarters decided to modernize the truck fleet and all drivers received brand new trucks. Sounds like a treat, doesn't it? Quite the contrary, the new panel trucks came with no opening from the cab (driver's area) into the storage compartment. As a result, the drivers' deliveries are more cumbersome. They now have to go outside into the elements and pull their products for delivery, the drivers cannot pull as close into tight loading docks, and they cannot hug curbs as close as they did in the past. This situation follows the opposite of the , 'if it ain't broke, don't fix it' philosophy. In this case the philosophy management showed was, 'It ain't broke, so let's fix it anyway.' As a result of the new trucks, the drivers are less motivated and less motivation means lower production. So instead of being a benefit to the drivers, the new trucks were a curse.

Tipping the COW: If corporate headquarters had the civility to ask the drivers to assess their current trucks, this situation could have been avoided. Here management acted like COWs.

Special note to those who are decision makers at businesses: Please don't just plan things out on paper without communicating with those who are on the front lines of the work. Things may look crystal clear on the drawing board but to those who perform the work function they might make no sense at all.

May I give another quick example? "Of course." (Says the omniscient third person writing voice.) "After all, it's your book." Thank you. A friend of mine works at a concession stand in a large arena. A corporate decision just came down that decreed that the concession stands will only be stocked with four (4) of the biggest selling items, large chocolate chip cookies, from now on before each event. It seems as though the employees at the arena loved the cookies as much as the crowds did so the arena employees bought large quantities of the yummy chocolate chip cookies, at full price, by the way; consequently the concession stands were always running short before event time. This typically left the stands with an average of four cookies before the start of each event, thus you can guess where the number, 4, came from. So, instead of the management deciding to increase the quantity of chocolate chip cookies, they decrease the amount so that the employees can't eat them all before the crowds arrive. This leaves the concession stands constantly scrambling during the events to stock more cookies. The result is that cookie sales are dramatically down at each concession stand, from a previous average of fifty (50) to now down to ten (10) cookies each night. Instead of some pencil pusher realizing that the company is in the business of selling cookies and the more the merrier, who cares whose mouth they go into, this decision maker focused into stopping that bad, hording gluttony of the employees. (sic) Of course, the wise corporate decision maker also doesn't realize that cutting off the pre-event treat for their workers may have some effect on morale and motivation.

Chapter Three
In Business...

Customer Service

Ever notice how customer service just doesn't exist in businesses any longer?

Bar patron, "Hey, Tim, put these beers and sandwiches on my tab."

Bartender, Yea...sure, but when are you going to pay that tab?"

Patron, waving a piece of paper, "Well, I've got the winning lottery ticket right here."

Bartender, "How much is the jackpot?"

Patron, "Two million."

Bartender, "That won't even cover it."

—-Robin Williams in a scene from the movie,

Good Will Hunting

Dr. John E. Mayer

An exchange such as the one above is pure Hollywood fiction in today's world of business. Running up a tab is certainly not in any course taught at Princeton business school. What does seem to be taught at business schools is the philosophy, <u>Get as much as you can as fast as you can by any means you can</u>.

To the new generation of business person customer service is an oxymoron. Customers are necessary evils to be tolerated but not encouraged. Businesses look upon customers like the stray dog that shows up in the alley. Don't give them the scraps you're throwing in the trash because you'll never get rid of them. People don't have value, they are objectified in the pursuit of the goal of obtaining more for the company.

Modern marketing strategy follows this philosophy of ditching customer service. After all, why worry about repeat customers when your goal is to sell to fifty million first time customers and then get out of the business.

A prime example of the rude behavior that rules in customer service is how business people talk to young people, people of color and minorities. In the case of young people, a parent tries to have young people learn how to handle their own business affairs only to have business people talk rude, short tempered, and to quickly dismiss any conversation with anyone 25 and under. A parent ends up handling the situation and miraculously the tone, attitude, and cooperation of the person changes immediately. Don't they realize that the parent is well aware of how their child was treated? The remedy here is to negotiate all the harder after hearing such a condescending attitude by this businessperson.

Similarly, people of color and minorities receive rude treatment by business people all the time. And again, once a Caucasian face or voice enters into the transaction, the tone changes immediately. COWs!

Customer service is so dead that it is the rare occasion today when a service person goes out of their way to help a customer. Those non-commission staff of retail stores treat customers as if the customer is imposing on their time to sell them the requested product. As a customer you are often greeted with a shrug of the shoulder, raised eyes, and an exhaled breath when approach the counter to pay for a product. There is rarely a friendly hello, a smile, and a thank you for your business. This type of service used to be commonplace, now it is a rare occasion.

The best example of this attitude of salespeople is drive-up windows at fast food restaurants. Nine out of ten times that you try and order at one of these windows, there is no way that you can understand what the voice on the other side of the microphone is saying. And it is not the fault of the microphone system. The restaurant allows staff to work the window when they do not know how to talk to people. (Youngsters, note, everyone complains about high school speech class but this is why speech class in high school is so important. Yea, everyone hates it, but you learn how to talk to other people in public. Pay attention in that class, many of you will be wearing that funny uniform and sticking your head out of a drive-up window for part of your life.)

Many people just hope and pray that what they receive somewhat resembles what they ordered. Drive-ups are supposed to be a convenience and not more of a hassle. At one very busy, very profitable McDonalds many people avoid the drive-up service altogether because it is notorious for having teens staff the drive-up window who cannot speak clearly. Mr. McDonalds, listen, you are losing money from these people. You could have changed your sign long ago to read, 'zillions served' if you just hired people who could speak clearly and say, 'Welcome to McDonalds' as if they half-heartedly meant it like the good ole' days.

Tipping the COW: Many people are too shy to utter the simple phrase, "I don't understand what you are saying. Please speak slowly and clearly." This phrase should be used whenever you encounter a person who can't speak English. Next, if you still don't understand the person behind the microphone, by pass the whole microphone thing and drive up to the window and talk to the person face-to-face. Often, it is easier to understand someone as you look at them. And you can delight in the response of the teenagers at the window as you break the corporate routine. As they look at you shocked that you didn't follow the drive-up rules, simply repeat, "I couldn't understand you. You need to talk clearly."

The connection has been lost between the individual customer and the individual worker's own personal gain from the customer. The largesse of business has taken this direct connection away. Workers don't get paid in response to serving the individual customer, but from serving the faceless company. Who cares if you provide poor service, they pay you just the same. Besides, there are plenty of customers out there. During a company's infancy when there are not as many customers, each person is valued. Each person was given respect because they represented personal gain.

Attorneys

The Mount Olympus of condescending attitudes is the legal profession. Lawyers are rude to everyone, young or old. An entire book can be written about the attitudes that lawyers inflict upon the public and I'm sure dozens have been written. Just let it be heard here that we have to stop reinforcing attorneys' bad manners.

It appears that somewhere in law school nice, polite, well-meaning young people get methamorphasized from the human race into the animal kingdom. They become COWs by the end of their third year in law school. Is there a class given on this?

Tipping the COW: If you look around, attorneys are plentiful and more are being churned out of school every term. If you must use one and they are treating you poorly, move on to the next one, it is as simple as that. WE have to stop reinforcing lawyers' bad COW manners. Only when we stop tolerating this behavior will these people change.

Let's take a lesson from how we are changing physicians' manners toward clients. Yes, this change is slow, but most patients now ask questions (God forbid!) about procedures and side effects, not settling for the old medical brush-off. Lawyers can be trained just as well. Enough said about lawyers.

Dr. John E. Mayer
The IRS

There has been all kinds of hype from the government about the 'new, taxpayer friendly' Internal Revenue Department. Don't believe a word of it. Like so many of today's businesses, the IRS is nice and friendly as long as you don't have a problem. If you have made a mistake, have a dispute with them, or missed a deadline, then their old tried and true colors come out as vicious as the old days.

This laughable ruse of the friendly IRS is best illustrated by a service they call the taxpayer advocate. This is supposed to be an ombudsman for the taxpayer who has had their job threatened or their home threatened by IRS action. First, if the IRS is now taxpayer friendly, then why would they be going around threatening homes and jobs? This doesn't seem to be too friendly to take away someone's job or home. This seems to be a basic contradiction.

This advocacy service is supposedly created for the taxpayer to be able to call on when their tax problem has reached these emergency situations. This service is a folly. Not only because of this inherent contradiction of this friendly agency taking away your job and home, but research also shows that there is a minimum wait of six weeks for an advocate to take your case. If you are losing your house or job, minutes and hours are precious let alone weeks. A minimum of six weeks is not going to save your home or job. This isn't a very friendly new service, it's a sham.

The words IRS and taxpayer advocate, taxpayer friendly, or any other positives coupled with those three initials will forever remain an oxymoron as long as such tactics are in place such as losing homes, jobs, or other significant essential life elements. The IRS is a supernova COW.

Tipping the COW: If you find yourself with a tax problem, run to the most reputable tax expert you can. Start with a CPA, either one you have used or a friend of a friend. This CPA should be a specialist in tax situations. Just apply the same rules on CPAs as you do with attorneys. If they treat you like dirt, run for the hills. CPAs often are disgruntled attorney wannabees. So, some of them copy the personality of attorneys because they emulate them so. If the CPA says you need an attorney, and you like the CPA, let them recommend one. If you are having a good experience with the CPA chances are that they will recommend someone who practices like they do.

Avoid those national tax resolution services. They are impersonal, have way too many clients and you will not get a feeling as though you have an ally. These services cannot give you the service that will give you peace of mind in the face of the nightmarish IRS monster.

Banks

Piggy banks shouldn't be the symbol of savings and indirectly of banks. The real symbol for banks should be COWwy banks. Banks ooze with COWish behavior. Many banks now charge a teller transaction fee when you physically go to a bank stand in line and wait for a teller and deposit money into the bank. Some banks have also started the practice of charging that same $1.50 for a deposit slip. How can banks justify charging $1.50 for going up to a teller and depositing money THAT THEY ARE GOING TO TURN AROUND AND MAKE LARGE AMOUNTS OF MONEY FROM?

Understand the economics of this. You give banks your money to use so that they can make large profits off it. Now, for the privilege of using our money for their advantage, they change us. Wasn't this called, 'double dipping' in the old days.

Everyone knows the old adage, 'People get loans that don't need the money'. What's the deal with these credit scores and impersonal technological formulas that don't allow for any civil treatment as explanation for life's circumstances? Let's treat people as people, with respect and dignity and not as numbers. If a bank would take this approach to people they would corner the market because it would be so refreshing to be treated like human beings and not formulas.

How do bankers avoid watching *It's a Wonderful Life* when it plays all day, every day during the holidays? Do bankers get the moral of that story? People prosper by being treated civilly. Gosh, Jimmy Stewart was even a banker in the movie. How much closer home does the message have to be? Jimmy Stewart gave loans to those who needed it. What a novel idea.

Tipping the COW: How many people just don't stand for these surcharges on their accounts. Try it. Look for accounts at banks that don't have these fees. Switch your money to banks that don't charge. With branch banking this shouldn't be a problem.

One can imagine what banks are pulling over on us if this very noticeable, audacious COW behavior is done right in front of our noses. Another tip for this COW is to check your bank statement every month and contest <u>every</u> fee they tack on. It doesn't matter if it is a standard fee, call anyway. If banks get enough calls questioning everything they may just get the message that they better treat us civilly.

The Phone Company

The COWish behavior of the phone company is also indicative of technology companies in general. My favorite COW of these companies behavior is trying to get customer service. You call and first it takes an ungodly amount of time to get through to someone which is interesting in itself for a communications business. Then in the process of solving the problem, which always takes several calls back to the company, you can never get the original person whom you talked to in the first place. Each time you call you must go through the nature of the problem, the history and what has been done thus far. What pencil pusher thought that this system was a more effective way to handle customer service? Why can't we be treated civilly and talk to the same person each time? I'll wait an extra moment to be connected with my original customer service agent just so I don't have to go through the 'story' every time I call. It is like going through an endless revolving door. You get so frustrated that you just want to give up with your trouble request. Ah ha, maybe that is why they put this system in place? They want us to get so frustrated that we give up our request for help.

Tipping the COW: If your problem takes more than one call ask for a supervisor right away. Get the supervisor's direct extension phone number. Keep very detailed notes on who you talked to and when. The supervisor must give you their name and extension. Now you have one person to help solve your problem and you have a direct number to them.

Insurance Companies

How long can insurance companies keep getting away with holding on to our money before they reimburse us? Do any of the people who work in insurance regulation ever use insurance? If they do they must suffer the same unnecessary delays that the general public does in order to get insurance reimbursements. Don't they think this is odd in the days of instant computer communication that we have to wait nine (9) months to get reimbursed for a pair of glasses that is covered by our group insurance plan? Try being late on paying your monthly premium and Voila! You get communication awful quick from the insurance company. But, nine months to one year waits for reimbursement are common.

Try being a health practitioner. Average claims are paid six months after services are rendered. Do the people who process these claims get a paycheck every week? Do they have any sensitivity to the fact that the insurance reimbursement is the provider's form of getting paid? Name another occupation that has to wait six months before getting paid for their labors. How do insurance companies think providers survive? What these delays in payments are doing is eliminating the existence of the private practitioner. A person who is in solo practice in health care cannot exist on not getting reimbursed for six months to one year.

Why don't healthcare providers take Medicare, Medicaid, Public Assistance patients? Because not only is the paperwork a nightmare, but the level of reimbursement is embarrassing. It is simply not economical to take on such patients. That means that low income patients get less than expert care because the best doctors will not take these cases.

The nightmare of paperwork was mentioned. The public thinks it is arrogant of providers to complain about doing paperwork, but let's take a look at the common sense of this issue. Let's say a provider charges $50.00 for an office visit. The provider spends one half hour directly caring for the patient. The provider spends $5.00 in office and medical supplies to treat what was ailing this person. The provider's office space, and other office expenses, including staff salaries, malpractice insurance, etc. add on an overhead cost of $18.00 for that one-half hour that the provider saw this patient. That leaves, $27.00, so far that the provider is being paid for their work. Now, add on another one half-hour of filling out insurance forms, completing office notes or charting on the patient, and follow-up insurance justification, a phone call from the insurance company to question the necessity of the treatment and any other paperwork that completes the requirements for caring for this simple visit. The result is that for a full hour of labor, the provider is paid conservatively $27.00. Sure, this is well above minimum wage, but think about what non-office expenses necessary for the provider to continue to practice must now come out of that $27, such as paying back school loans, association memberships, etc. Let's take away another $5.00 from that visit to pay these personal expenses related to being a provider. Now think about how many other, less valued occupations in our society get paid much, much more than this. The provider is actually selling their time and knowledge. When a provider has to spend extra time filling out insurance company justifications to get $23.00 and they will not get paid that money for six months, you can see why providers are angry about filling out paperwork. Would a union bricklayer volunteer without being paid to fill out a half hour of paperwork in order to lay one half-hour of bricks? I think not.

On the other side of this issue, the insurance companies have adopted their COWish practices because in an earlier time in healthcare, the Cows who were doctors abused the system and this necessitated the implementation of the COW mentality in the insurance business.

For example, one psychiatrist used to be called the, "minute man" by the staff at the hospital where he practiced. They called him this because he would visit his patients in the hospital and the staff would count the time he would spend with the patient for this hospital visit. To the staff's disgust, he would be out of the room within a minute for each patient. The psychiatrist charged the insurance company $150.00 for each of these 'hospital consultations'. This psychiatrist did not even maintain an outpatient practice (Too much overhead.) instead hospitalized every person who came to his care. He didn't even know what psychotherapy or medication management meant. To this day he practices in the same manner. I'm sure his paperwork is flawless.

Tipping the COW: Legislation should be enacted that mandates insurance reimbursement to be made in three (3) weeks and if it isn't, then considerable interest and penalties should be paid to the provider. Suggest such a bill be advanced to your senator or congressman. They would love to have a bill they can trumpet as a cause.

Delivery Companies

Remember the efficiency expert at the technology companies that figured out how to improve customer service by giving you a new person to talk to each time you call in about your trouble? Well, this same guy was probably hired by delivery companies to figure out that they can't just give you a time range in which your package will be delivered. Again, with modern technology, these companies can't figure out that your area's delivery person is at your building approximately within a half-hour of the same time every day? It doesn't take a rocket scientist to figure out that unless they start to give narrower ranges of delivery time, then the delivery has to be made over and over again costing them more overhead. It is not just about treating the public more civilly, it doesn't make economic sense to act like a COW.

Tipping the COW: Your area should have a standard delivery time for each company. This way you and the company can depend on when a package will arrive. This will eliminate re-delivery. With all the rest of the information that is filed on the computer can't delivery companies save your delivery time preferences using your address?

Doing our job

One of the most uncivilized acts we can perform is not doing our own work with honor. In the aftermath of 9-11-01 as the stories unfold about the flight schools that reported unqualified suspicious characters taking jet aircraft training to the airport security people who nap while dangerous objects pass through the scanners if people did their job with integrity could we have prevented 9-11? The famous psychologist Erick Erickson theorized that the highest form of social maturity that one can attain is when they perform their best as an individual. In this way society benefits as each person tries to be the best person they can. This theory should be the goal of each American worker. The New York City terrorist attack should teach us that each job in this country is vital and when not performed to its utmost people will get hurt.

COWs don't take their jobs seriously. They perform their jobs as if the job was about them rather than looking at the larger picture.

Tipping the COW: Tipping this COW is in the hands of employers. Employers must strive to instill a motivation in employees on the importance of their work. Companies should be able to fire those employees that don't work by this standard.

But all of us should take this responsibility as well. When you see someone not doing the job they are supposed to do, call them on it. A simple, "Do your job…" will suffice. If you get a bad reaction, no reaction, or some retaliation for your comment, let that person's supervisor know what is happening and then say to the supervisor, "Do your job!"

The Myth of Technical Support

Recently, I had trouble with a computer. I liked the features it had and one in my price range with comparable features was hard to find. The manufacturer of this computer was one of the major brand names and I had owned several of their products before.

The computer's modem didn't work from the day I bought it. I took it back to my retailer and they gave me another model. Same problem occurred. I took it back again and again received a replacement with no questions asked. This is a terrific national retailer. I took the computer home and the modem still didn't work. I was too embarrassed to make a fourth trip to the retailer so I decided to call the technical support people at the large computer manufacturer. It was at this point that the real circus began.

Of course, each time one calls the technical support the wait time is intolerable. You then encounter the system mentioned previously. Upon each call, you must get a new technician and they have to hear you problem all over again. Then they all try first exactly what the previous technician tried thinking they took an extra DeVry course that the previous technician skipped. I then discovered a well kept secret. The technicians who handle your call first are all what the company calls a 'first level' technician. The first level technician has about enough knowledge to check whether you

Dr. John E. Mayer

have the machine plugged in correctly and if you know how to turn it on. Nonetheless, these first level technicians all want to play Scotty on the USS Enterprise and fix the problem even though it is way over their heads. So you have to spend countless phone calls and painful hours with these people until they give up and transfer you to a 'second level' technician. These people do not wear Star Trek pins on their shirts and are at least two years out of DeVry but they still dream of someday working at a Radio Shack. Once with the second level technicians, the process just starts all over again. Tell the story, try everything everyone else did, fail, and you guessed it, get transferred to the 'third level' technician. When this level fails, then they transfer you to the corporate engineering department. One would think that these would be the people who put these machines together, but they are only people who <u>did</u> work at Radio Shack and left because they can't communicate with people.

Try talking to an electronics technician. At one point I was told to get a part for the computer. Instead of just telling me the part name and where to get it, the corporate engineer had to read me the two pages of technical specifications he pulled up on the internet and finally told me the name of the part and, of course, it would be available at my local Radio Shack.

After the corporate engineer couldn't fix the problem I simply ended the frustration of this ring-around-the-rosy game and exchanged the computer for another brand. I don't like the features near as much, but I don't have to call an engineer every day of my life.

Tipping the COW: Use my experience. If you have to call more than once, ask for an upper level technician right away. Don't tell your story

38

over and over again. Let them read the notes. Take notes for yourself and don't allow them to do every step the last person failed at. If you cannot understand the speech of the person over the phone ask for someone you can understand preferably a supervisor right away. Begin that conversation with the supervisor with the statement, "I couldn't understand the technician whom I was talking with so I asked for you." Maybe if we say this enough we will not have to suffer through a person who cannot communicate because they will begin to hire people who have phone skills as well as some technical knowledge.

Chapter Four
At the Doctor's Office…

Waiting

Can some office manager explain how patients have to wait two hours for a visit that is given a set appointment time? How is this justified? And how does the public continue to put up with such nonsense? The public is being told from a variety of sources to have more of a consumer attitude about health care, yet the basic doctor-patient relationship has not changed. You wouldn't wait in this manner for any other service you purchase.

<u>Tipping the COW</u> Start a habit of giving doctors fifteen minutes. If your appointment is at the hour and your not waited on (Yes, 'waited on' is the appropriate phrase.) by a quarter past the hour, then politely tell the receptionist you are leaving and want to reschedule this appointment for a time when you will be waited on promptly. Use that phrase, "I want to return when I can be waited on as scheduled." Sure you are sick, but you will feel worse if you wait an inordinate length of time. If you really want to get this office to pay attention, ask the receptionist where is the nearest emergency care service or outpatient facility (Physicians call them, Doc-in-the-box.)

All of this and you haven't seen the doctor yet. Now the doctor arrives and she or he has the personality of a dead fish. No hello or we get the politician's sincerity in the doctor's tone of voice. And the public makes all kinds of rationalizations for this insulting behavior. "He's (she's) so busy." "I'd rather have her (him) be smart than polite." "I'm not paying them to be nice, I just want them to fix me." These rationalizations are absolutely nonsense. They just propagate bad manners in these people. Let's stop this nonsense. Doctors can be the world's biggest COWs.

Doctor's Attitude

In medical school young doctors-to-be copy their professorial mentors' attitude toward patients. Traditionally patients are dehumanized by doctors as a coping mechanism against the attachment to a patient with whom they have to observe suffering. The thinking was that if a doctor became emotionally attached to the patient, then they cannot objectively care for that patient. Get too close to the suffering and the doctor will get consumed by the suffering and not make decisions in the best interest of the healing of the patient. The problem is that this coping mechanism was adopted centuries ago and we now know better ways to cope with the hardships of others. Doctors need to learn better ways to cope with pain and suffering and not just behave the way they do because their teachers behave that way.

41

At one prominent medical school in the late 70's, a study was commissioned by the medical school deans to determine why this school was graduating physicians with poor, cynical attitudes toward patients. This was a noble endeavor for this or any medical school to undertake.

A brilliantly designed study researched this question. This study analyzed every facet of medical school education, ranging from the process of choosing students to studying retired physicians. After years of study the result determined that physician's personalities change as a result of the physician models they experience in medical school. Of course, this was not the result that the medical school anticipated or wanted. The study ended up in the infamous circular file. The once progressive aim of the medical school was to hear it was the lure of money, or the demands of the public, or the people they chose to enter medical school. They wanted to hear anything but themselves. So, along with the results, the remediation of the problem was also dumped.

Tipping the COW: Call a doctor on their attitude. Let them know that they are treating you rudely. Demand customer service. Doctors provide a service, a service you are paying for so demand good customer service just like you would and should with anyone from whom you purchase services. Please stop treating doctors and their staff any different.

Medical Staff

The lack of civility is not restricted to the doctors. Receptionists, nurses, accountants, office managers and other staff that man doctor's offices, hospitals, and clinics all copy the doctor's lead and treat the patients (customers) with the same lack of civility. The spread of these bad manners does not follow some epidemiological pattern; it is simply systems theory in action. In a system the head or leader of the system, in this case the doctors, sets the philosophical and practical tone for the whole system. So if the doctor acts like an ass, you can bet that everyone from there on down will act that way also. Using this knowledge one can also look out for situations that will put you in compromising situations. If you go to a doctor's office, hospital or clinic and the gatekeepers treat you in a rude, uncivil, manner, you can bet that once you see the doctor, he will treat you the same way.

Tipping the COW: Only choose doctors and their offices that make you feel welcome and caring. After all, being sick is no fun, don't compound it by people who make you feel worse. If a doctor or one of their staff treats you poorly change doctors immediately and stiff them for their bill. Just write across it, 'Service not delivered.'

Receptionists

No one trains receptionists anymore. Receptionists are the first to greet customers, visitors, guests and potential customers, yet they often have the personality style that turns people off rather than invite people in. Their attitude is often one of self-importance and ownership. It is as if they own the business they are gate keeping. The result is that the public is turned off from the start of whatever institution you are entering. The consequences of that attitude has a ripple effect on what happens next as you enter the place.

As an example, recently my wife and I went to visit a friend in the hospital. She had just delivered a baby. When we arrived at the hospital, certainly in a good mood at this joyous occasion we were greeted by the maternity hospital Nazi. The receptionist barked commands at us, scowled as we signed in and in general turned a happy entrance into a confused, unwelcome cloud over our head. As we entered the maternity floor and walked past other staff we couldn't help but wait to be yelled at or told to go home. We felt like we were intruding upon the hospital staff while we entered. Of course, our mood changed as soon as we saw our friend and her baby.

Tipping the COW: Let people in charge know how you were made to feel by these gatekeepers. Don't stand for being treated poorly by a greeter. If those in charge won't listen, then go higher up. Just don't make a confrontation with the receptionist, they won't care or listen or change without pressure from above.

Patient Rights

As much as modern medicine has been advised to disclose to the public the side effects of medications, few doctors thoroughly advise patients of the side effects of the medications they are receiving.

The biggest offenders in this last act are mental health care providers. Psychotropic drugs (Those prescribed for emotional regulation.) are the most widely prescribed drugs of all. Psychotropic drugs can and do have very serious side effects yet many of these side effects are minimized when a patient is prescribed these drugs. Like to feel less depressed? Take this, but sorry, you will also lose your sexual libido. Feeling anxious? We can fix that, but I forgot to mention that you may have some suicidal thoughts after taking this. Oh, your kid talks back to you, here have her take this, but it may just make her as high as a kite because it is a stimulant after all.

Providers of all kinds in mental health can be COWs. They act like COWs because they think you are a lesser person than they are because you are suffering from mental turmoil. This is just another form of COW syndrome as these health care people feel that they don't have your problems. What difference is this from, "I'm better than you are?" None.

Mental hospitals are particular COWs. And who are their biggest victims? Youth, of course, young people are indiscriminately hospitalized every day under misrepresented pretenses. An example will best illustrate how uncivilized our society treats young people in this regard.

A seventeen-year-old high school student gets himself rip roaring drunk at a party. He passes out. A rite of passage in his social group when a drinker passes out is that someone shaves off half of one of the helpless drinker's eyebrows. On this occasion, our passed out teen suddenly wakes up from his stupor only to open his eyes to one of his peers straddled across his body and wielding a glistening razor blade moving toward his left eye. Even from his inebriated state the teen bolts up and violently attacks the peer on top of him. In the process the razor leaves a gaping wound across the cheek of the seventeen-year-old. The wound inflames the teen even more, now other teens at the party have joined in the out-of-control fracas. Soon it evolves into an all out brawl and the police arrive to break things up. Our seventeen-year-old now consumed by rage and still drunk is taken to a psychiatric hospital by the police. Once at the hospital, the teen is placed in full leather restraints, given a major tranquilizer and kept over night. The boy's parents are told that he will only be kept over night until he calms down.

The next morning at 6:30 am a staff psychiatrist who barely speaks English comes into his room to 'examine' him. He was still in restraints, had slept for an hour and one half in his tattered clothes, his wound was poorly bandaged, he had vomited on himself and was still under the influence of the tranquilizer. The psychiatrist spends a total of five minutes with the boy and prescribes a heavy dose of Depekote, a mood stabilizer. When the mother called and was told the boy was going to receive this drug, she asked if there were any side effects and the nurse stated that the boy would only feel drowsy. Never informing her of the range of other possible side effects. Psychiatric hospitals are based on lies and deception that is why insurance companies are reimbursing them less and less. Is this the way to treat people with problems? Oh, there are a few around the country that are fair and decent, but they are not in my community and I doubt they are in yours.

Better solution? Don't put this boy in a psychiatric hospital. He's a drunk. Call the police, let him sleep in lock-up for the night and the next day find a therapist who specializes in teens and families and work out a system that corrects this boy's problems and habits. This is civil treatment for this boy and this family. Sheriff Andy of Mayberry had the right approach. He locked up the town drunk, Otis, let him sleep it off and then spent the rest of the episode trying to solve Otis's family problems.

It is no wonder why mental health care continues to be saddled by stereotypes and prejudice. The vast majority of the mental health care givers are inadequate. This is a field where the tools of the trade are the mind, emotions and personality of the caregiver, yet it is flooded with people who have the personality of a librarian on Quaaludes. This is a profession that should be as anti-COW as any, but the public is subjected to an abundance of COWS. It seems that mental health providers cope with this field by considering those who come for help as inferior.

Of Course, another problem facing mental health's reputation with the general public is that it staffs its clinics and agencies with people who are poorly trained and possibly not able to work in other branches of health care. Mental health care is considered unscientific, (translate as—easy) even by those inside the field and as a result many staff positions are filled with people who are not capable and many just plain not bright.

Tipping the COW: When seeking mental health services the public needs to be particularly sensitive to aspects of the caregiver's manner, intelligence and personality that seem not to be in harmony with theirs or that just don't make any sense.

A perfect example of this warning comes from a friend who is one of the thousands of outstanding mental health practitioners in the United States. My friend is a gifted therapist with a Ph. D. from a major university. Several years ago a new client came into his office looking for help. This male client looked and presented himself like the actor Mickey Rourke in a bad mood.

Further, the client was a successful business owner in a chain of stores in the auto industry, yet by the grease permanently embedded under his finger nails and in the creases of his bear-like hands even Sherlock Holmes' bubbling friend Watson could deduce that either this man was a self-made man, still pitched in with the gritty work of his business, or both. He certainly gave the impression of anything but an introspective, new age aficionado. The client was looking for help with a marital problem he had for seven years. In evaluating the history of the case, my friend asked the routine question of whether or not the client had sought any mental health help prior to this appointment. Much to my friend's surprise the client shot back, "Sure."

My friend then asked innocently, "Could you tell me about that?"

With that question, the client went on to describe, "Oh, yea I've been goin' to this shrink for four years, twice a week."

Incredulously my friend, had to ask, "Haven't you mentioned this marital problem to him?"

"Sure…" He said. "Sure, the first session I mentioned it to him, but he said the best overall treatment for me would be for me to regress. So, he had me strip down to my underwear and lie on the floor in a fetal position and scream for forty-five minutes. So, I've been doing that twice a week for four years."

Dumbfounded, my friend, dared to ask, "You mean you and he never talked…never discussed issues?

"We said hello, I assumed the position and commenced to scream, finished said goodbye and then left."

"Didn't you ever question this approach or the fact that you were not getting better?" he asked.

The man responded weakly, "No."

Tipping the COW: If your therapist isn't someone you would feel comfortable passing on the street, then go somewhere else. Get referrals for therapists from people you trust who have personal knowledge of the therapist. Don't go to agencies or through services. Try a therapist, if you are not getting better, stop, and go somewhere else.

Chapter Five
At the Health Club...

Cleaning up After Themselves

How come people cannot pick up their used towels? They leave them lying on the floor, in the shower, in lockers, everyplace but in the towel bin. Do they expect mom to pick up after them?

Tipping the COW: As you walk past the lazy fellow member with your used towels in hand, point to the floor where their towels lay with no intention of making it to the towel bin. Politely say, "I'm taking my towels to the bin, would you like me to take yours as well?"

God forbid that a member cleans a sink after they use it. Men are the worst offenders. Ever see the condition of a sink after a man has shaved? Hair stubble, water, shaving cream smeared all over the counter. Is it unmanly to clean up after yourself? Is it possible that they think that their membership excludes them from cleaning up after themselves? Is this not macho? What is the rule here? What suffering woman raised these little princes?

Remedy, take some soap and neatly write on the mirror, 'Please clean up after yourself- a fellow member'. This personal plea from a member rather than the staff may call more attention to the ill mannered.

Care of Equipment

Try using a piece of equipment after someone. It is probably full of sweat when the civil thing to do would be to wipe it off after you were done.

How do you like the people who sit on equipment and read, talk and are oblivious to the fact that you want to use the equipment they are wasting away at.

Tipping the COW: Don't be afraid to ask these goldbricks to move. People seem to think they can't ask others to move off a piece of equipment. Doing so is perfect health club etiquette. If a person is dallying simply ask, "May I use this?" You pay your dues also. But, expect a sigh, raised eyebrows or some other sign that you are inconveniencing the COW.

In clubs where there is a TV or stereo how many ignorant people just change the station without asking around if anyone minds? The COW doesn't even think to ask if anyone else has been listening to a station. They change the channel as if they own the television. They don't even consider that anyone else would possibly object. After all, no one else in world matters to the COW.

Tipping the COW: Even if you could care less about what was on the TV, object to the COW changing it without asking. Do this just for the practice.

It's called a—WORKOUT—this should mean you do your WORK and then get—OUT!

Loud, Obnoxious Behavior

Of course my favorite COW behavior in health clubs are the 'noise machines'. These are not pieces of equipment, but people who assume no one else is bothered by their grunts and groans, yelps and screeches as they perform their grueling circuit of power walking with two pound weights on the treadmill. There is a fellow in Chicago who exercises at the health club next door to the Chicago Board of Trade who is notorious for this type of behavior. As he grinds through his Stairmaster workout he literally yells at the top of his lungs. His cries can be heard outside the doors of the health club. I have seen people frightened to enter because of this oaf's behavior. Of course, none of the health club staff say a word to this fellow, because he is supposedly some wealthy trader from the Chicago Board of Trade.

Tipping the COW: Do the staff think he is going to put them in his will if they treat him with deference? So he is wealthy, is he any different from anyone else who pays the same dues? He is a COW and a nuisance. It is time that the management of these clubs put a stop to this pandering.

This brings me to a very key concept about the COW syndrome. That is, the rest of society often contributes to this behavior because we reinforce it with our complacency. The oaf at the Board of Trade health club is a prime example. It is the duty of staff people to ensure an environment conducive to working out. To do so means not only keeping the equipment clean, picking up the towels, straightening the weights in the weight rack, but to approach a COW like this goof and inform him to consider that his bellowing is a hindrance to someone else's workout and he should tone it down.

Children at Health Clubs

People should bring children into health clubs. There are hordes of reasons why this is a great idea for a family. What a wonderful way to model a healthy lifestyle. It is also a great way to spend time with your kids while you are pursuing something that is so healthy for you. The problem lies in this last point. Spending time with your kids. So many people come to the health club with their children only to have the kids running all around unattended while the parent goes about their workout almost oblivious to the needs of the children and of course oblivious to the needs of the other adults in the health club.

If parents are bringing children to the health club then they should exercise with them and not leave them to play by themselves. There are plenty of vigorous activities that an adult can participate in with children. They should do those activities and not try to workout as if they are not there. One would assume that the purpose of bringing the children to the health club would be to participate in an activity together, but the COW parent wants the children to be occupied as if they are in day care while

53

they selfishly go about their workout. This is rude and selfish behavior on the part of the parent.

Tipping the COW: Remedy, health clubs should promote activities that families can participate in together. If they don't have such activities then suggest that they create them. The clubs will find these parent/child activities will bring more members into the clubs and thus increase memberships. This may also take some orientation for families so that they can learn how to enjoy the club together. Clubs should do this type of orientation when the family signs up for the club services.

Sporting Events

The loudmouths who insist on yelling profanities and other negatives in crowded sporting events need to be escorted from the games. At most sporting events one finds people of all ages, races, and walks of life. It is a mirror to the decay of our civility that the crowd behaves with no respect to this fact. These behaviors only occur because these spectators have no concern about the other fans at the event. They are COWs.

A favorite example of the primitive behavior at sporting events came several years ago at a NFL football game in Chicago between the Chicago Bears and the visiting Detroit Loins. The game took place at Soldier Field in Chicago. I took my young son to see his first live sporting event. An occasion that is sadly not possible any longer with the outrageous costs of attending any professional sporting event. We had decent seats that had been labeled with the paradoxical designation of, 'reserved'. Paradoxical because as you will see they were certainly not reserved for any one with any semblance of humanity. As we took our seats we couldn't help to notice that there were a row of Catholic nuns sitting several rows in front of us. They were particularly distinctive because they wore light blue habits. This was the same colors of the hated visiting Detroit Lions Football Team. As the game progressed, not only were these nuns dressed in the offending colors but the crowd became aware that they were indeed true to their colors and were Detroit Lions fans. Once that discovery was made all bedlam broke loose from the Chicago fans that were in proximity to the nuns. The Chicago fans threw popcorn, candy, gum, anything at the nuns. The F word was directed at them anytime the Chicago team did anything remarkable. Taunts of , "Go home, penguins," and "Pray for that, sister," bellowed out continually.

My son and I were not the only Dad and son combinations in the area, but the COWs had no concern what effect they were having on the children in their proximity. Their only concern was their own pleasure. True, in the wool COWs.

If such behavior is acceptable in public, would these COWs display such behavior elsewhere, let's say in church…Yeah! It's the F….ing Lamb of God…all right…Whoa!…Satin, you suck!…Condemn this you bastard!

Tipping the COW: Ushers are now policing the crowd more aggressively for smoking. Start policing the crowd with the same vigor for obnoxious behavior. And what about obnoxious behavior around the stadiums? Doesn't the municipality have the obligation to police these crowds as they exit the stadium and hoard into the surrounding communities?

The Wrigley Field neighborhood was mentioned in a previous chapter for their COWish behavior, but one legitimate gripe they do have, like all communities that sit adjacent to these stadiums, is that their should be better crowd control as these COWs enter and exit the stadium. Ask residents next to stadiums how many people they catch urinating on their property? Ringing their doorbells? Destroying their landscaping? Given the price of tickets for these events, now upwards of $100 each, one would think that these events draw a more civilized crowd than the homeless and mentally impaired who feel it is their right to urinate on the side of someone's house just because they guzzled too many $8 beers at a sporting event?

Public Restrooms

This crude behavior wasn't confined to the stands. If you have not been in a public men's room at a sports stadium, it is an eye opening experience. Crude language, vile, sexist jokes, primitive comments about body parts, and inappropriate adoration of beer all fill the air. My starkest memory of men's room behavior at a stadium came again at that NFL game at half time. While waiting in a long line to use the toilets men were urinating on the walls of the bathroom, in the sinks that lined the walls before the urinals, and in their beer cups. All the while bragging with the most obnoxious male braggadocio about urinating and being "guys".

As a father taking my son to his first "adult" sporting event it was a total embarrassment. We never returned to another football game.

Rude restroom behavior is not confined to sports stadiums. The modern restroom still has its roots in that smelly, filthy grandparent called the, outhouse. As such, people treat restrooms as if they are outhouses transplanted into malls, restaurants, public buildings, etc. They are often just as filthy as the old outhouses. At any given time there are paper towels thrown all around, unflushed toilets, and water, water everywhere.

Tipping the COW: Treat a public washroom as you would one in your home. Missed the garbage can with your used paper towel? Then pick it up and dispose it properly. And I can't imagine how someone leaves a toilet unflushed at these public washrooms. Do they not flush toilets in their homes? I would betcha that that is not the case. I can't imagine anyone adorning their bathrooms with toilets that have feces floating freely. Flushing toilets is a habitual response at home so how come so many public toilets remain unflushed. Can't the stadium, sports team or city station an usher in these restrooms to maintain decency and order?

Chapter Six
Transportation...

Driving

Since 1982 the time one spends in their car in traffic is up 236%. The average driver spends the equivalent of one full work week each year in traffic. The average mom spends 66 minutes each day driving. This time out of mom's day is more time than the average mom spends playing with her child and it is even more time than she spends dressing, feeding, and bathing her child. For the modern family, the car is often the only place where conversation takes place. The automobile does provide parents with a captive audience where parents can attempt to get the family's attention.

We don't just socialize in our cars, we dine from drive-through fast food restaurants, and we are entertained by radios, CD players, even TV's. We are virtually living in our vehicles and you would think that with all this effort to make the auto our second home that people's behavior while in their vehicle would mimic that of how they should act in their own home. Instead, people behave while driving as if they are invisible to others. Two thousand pounds of metal makes most people feel totally incubated from other people so they don't have to consider that there is another person in the other hunk of metal. These moving metal protective enclosures give those inside the illusion that no one else exists outside of their little metal world. It is no wonder that so much COW behavior takes place while driving.

Turn Signals

Why can't people figure out how to use the turn signal in their cars? Not only don't people use turn signals, but when the minority of people do use signals, they click them on while they are already into their turn. What good does that do for the motorists behind you? The turn signal is best used well ahead of your turn so that you may signal those drivers behind you for convenience and safety. Although a courtesy, the turn signal is primarily a safety device, to let other drivers know you are making a maneuver with a 2,000 pound machine that can cause great harm when used recklessly.

Tipping the COW: As you pass a turning car that is not using their signal, give a polite blast of your horn and then make a flashing sign with your hand. This lets the driver know why you are honking and frustrated.

Tailgaters

What are drivers accomplishing by driving on your tail so closely. You're going sixty in the far left-hand lane of a highway and another car pulls up so close that you can see the other driver's nose hairs in your rear-view mirror. He or she then blinks the lights off and on repeatedly. What is this supposed to mean? Sure, the tailgater wants this to mean get out of my way and let me speed past you to a state of asphalt Nirvana, of course, they are COWs and you are in their precious space in the world. But, you're doing nothing offensive and may be comfortable cruising in this lane at a reasonable and legal speed. They're wrong, so what do you do?

Tipping the COW: The most effective way of handling this situation is not the most satisfying. For the most part you would like to slow down to a crawl, block the tailgater in and smile through your rearview mirror with a big Cheshire cat grin. Doing this will only make matters worse for you as this idiot flashes his headlights all the more furiously and tailgates all the closer. Better suggestion is to pull over immediately at the first flash of tailgater headlight then pick up your cell phone (Yea, we all have them.) and report the car's license plate to the police as a driver recklessly out of control on the highway. Then you can pass him up with glee as the officer has stopped him to read his fortune.

Stop Signs

In keeping with the "I'm the Center-Of-the-World syndrome" people are increasingly speeding through red lights, not stopping at stop signs, and of course, turning from the far lane, cutting across all traffic and making their turn. For COWs the laws don't apply to them. (So they think.) They can't understand why they should obey a law when they will not be punished for it.

Then we have the Hollywood stoppers. Those people whose right-of-way is so much more important than the rest of ours that they stop for a millisecond at a four way stop, hardly pausing, when you have been there for minutes. What COWs!

But we do know that these COWs probably understand the difference between 'stop' and 'slow down'. Just start hitting one in the head and ask, "Do you want me to—stop—or –slow down?"

Tipping the COW: The best solutions are the same as suggested for the tailgater, memorize the license plate number and then call 911 and report a reckless driver. In fact, put that 911 number on the speed dial option of your cell phone. And don't forget to get the license plate number of these jerks. You may think this is a wasted effort because the police will be informed after the fact but, a fundamental characteristic of COWs is that they will repeat the behavior so the police may just spot this person farther down the road doing the same thing. That's when they nab 'em.

Littering

People who throw their garbage out of the window are enormous COWs. They are placing road hazards on the pavements. Call them in! Let the police deal with them. That is the police's job. Listen, the police in your community may not respond at the drop of a hat to each one of these situations, but at the very least you have the satisfaction of knowing that you may have made their life difficult.

Do you know what city is considered to have the cleanest streets? Its is Singapore. That's because the police actually take the littering laws seriously. Let's all start to encourage the police to take these laws seriously.

Tipping the COW: Call the police on litterers. If they get enough calls, then maybe they will see how serious the public is upset about these conditions. Calling your local politician's office accomplishes the same goal. If the police are unresponsive, calling your local politician's office may be even more effective.

Let's encourage our communities to restart those anti-littering campaigns. What ever happened to that American Indian with the tear running down his cheek? That sure left an impression on me. I still remember it.

Another place instruction about littering should take place is in schools. It is here where we can have the most impact. Schools should encourage students to pick up papers on the floor, clean up after themselves in the cafeteria, etc. If schools made littering a part of their disciplinary code, that is a student gets a detention if caught littering, this leaves life-long impressions on the importance of littering.

Finally, how about giving the homeless a few bucks for picking up litter? Communities can distribute garbage bags to the homeless and then give them a few bucks for every full bag they bring back. Have some monitors ride around to make sure they are picking up garbage off the street and not just raiding dumpsters and voila', you have a cleaner community. But, some politician will scream that we will offend the unions if we install such a program. Well, offer union garbage collectors the same exact deal. How many $37.50 an hour union garbage collectors do you think will take their free garbage bag and spend their free time getting $2.00 per bag? End of union objection.

Turning

Don't you love the people who are ever so slowly coasting to a stop. These COWs don't realize that they are blocking the car behind them from efficiently approaching the right hand corner and turning thus reducing the congestion for all. They see a stop light up ahead and then slow down to a crawl thinking they are reducing the world's consumption of oil by letting their car coast to the light. But they are not considering the vehicles behind them that can get out of the way of those behind them, thus reducing gridlock which <u>does</u> reduce fuel costs directly.

Tipping the COW: Not only beep your horn, but use your turn signal and wave your hand to let them know you need to turn.

The Universal Sign of Friendship

People give the universal sign of friendship (the middle finger) as easily as they blink an eye. This seems to happen more when driving than anywhere else. Does this really mean anything anymore? When someone 'flips you off' do you really care? This act has been so overused that it just doesn't have any effect anymore. But COWs are slow to change because, as the center of the world they are often oblivious to the changes in the world around them. So COWs continue to use this antiquated device. They are such COWs that they don't realize that it might be more effective if they actually did something that took some effort, like mooning you.

Tipping the COW: I have started to blow fellow motorists a kiss when they salute me with that harmless signal, the middle finger. Try it. The reaction from the hapless COW giving the salute will either be confusion, increased anger, silence, embarrassment, or amusement. Any of which will be more effective than flipping back the bird. You'll really get a rise out of the other drivers with this and you'll get even a bigger response if the other driver is of the same sex.

Classic Driving Rudeness

Of course, then there are the classics: people who drive slow in the left hand lane on the expressway, trucks that use the left hand lane on expressways, trucks that drive on weight restricted roads when the alternative would take a few minutes more and double parking all over the place.

Of the classics, it appears as if delivery trucks that must double-park when ten feet away are large gapping holes of curb space is a favorite of beer trucks for some reason. Possibly, the beer truck drivers feel that the odds are in their favor since the vast majority of Americans are beer drinkers and will forgive the liberties that their pushers (pardon me, suppliers) indulge in. Take heed, Fed Ex drivers are catching up fast in this category.

Tipping the COW: Yea, get the license plate number, the type of truck, the time of day and the location where it was making the delivery. Oh, also get the name of the beer distributor that they are employed by. This company name is printed on the side of the driver's cab door. All of this information will save you time and headaches hunting their employer down. Then call the truck's employer. Why do all this? I'll bet you will get a reward like a case of beer for your actions. Heck, call in every delivery truck you see double parked and you might just create a cottage industry for yourself with all the free products and services you get as rewards.

Changing Lanes

Can there be any better example of disregard for other drivers and driving as if you are the only car in the world than those drivers who cross over three lanes to try and turn a corner or make their exit on an expressway?

Tipping the COW: This example of COW behavior happens so quickly that there are not many remedies available to you. The only suggestion that can be made is to take your mobile phone, memorize or copy down the license plate number and call the police about the offender. Heck, it may not lead to any consequences for that driver but you wouldn't know if it did anyway as you would be far away from the offender. Calling the police will at least give you the satisfaction of fantasizing that the police did, in fact, apprehend the offender and throw the book at them.

Just like the multilane changer another 'in-your-face' driving behavior are the drivers who insist on changing lanes by slowing down almost to a complete stop. Didn't these people take driver's education in school. It is unsafe to change lanes by slowing way down and then pulling into the next lane. Good, courteous driving means that you merge into the next lane by keeping pace with the moving traffic. You do this by anticipating your change of lane and then merging at a safe speed.

Tipping this COW: You guessed it. Get on that phone and call in a driver recklessly changing lanes. When you make these calls make them sound very serious. Let the police know that this is a potentially dangerous situation and someone is about to get hurt.

Horns

How about those beeping horns? Why do we even need them in vehicles any more? Except for the uses we have talked about in this chapter, horns are ineffective by themselves. You need to accentuate your horn blowing with some creative hand gestures that let the other driver know why you are frustrated. If you lamely just toot your horn it gets no response from the COWs. If you are gesturing frantically, people tend to pay more attention. Some time ago horns had the effect of the middle finger on fellow motorists. Now, they mean absolutely nothing and quite frankly, I would rather have a few bucks off my purchase price rather than have this vestigial organ. I gesture and get someone's attention some other way.

I would really like to see automakers come up with a more advanced method of communication at other motorists rather than the impotent horns that equip current cars. How about loud speakers in every car? This way you can express exactly how you feel about the other drivers. And, you can tell errant drivers exactly what they did wrong. The horn, circa Henry Ford and the Model T, is one piece of car equipment that just has not been updated since those early days. Let's come up with something that really offends the other driver when they do their self-indulgent maneuvers. Nobody cares anymore about getting the horn, the finger, the stare, the glare or other car signals. Detroit, Japan, Germany give us some tools against the COWs.

The annoyance of the horn is epitomized by the car owner behind you that has to lay on their horn when you do not move off the changed light in a millisecond or you do not turn the corner fast enough as you wait for pedestrians walking across the street.

Tipping the COW: When this latter situation happens just take all the more time to make your maneuver with your vehicle.

Pedestrians vs Vehicles

Speaking of walking across the street, how threatening is it to be walking across a street with the clear right-of-way and a turning car speeds its way around the corner and pushes so close to you that it all but touches you. Or a car races around the corner and zooms into a turn right in front of you narrowly missing you by millimeters. These are examples of how COWs drive a vehicle. Is that COW's moment of time so precious to the driver that it is worth frightening you or harming you? For COWs, the answer is yes. They do feel that their time is so precious that your well-being just doesn't matter. In fact, you can tell that a COW is behind the wheel by the way an individual drives in this selfish, inconsiderate manner.

It used to be that there was an unwritten law that pedestrians have the right of way under any circumstance. Today, with the United States being the fast-food society that it is, everyone is in a hurry-up mode so pedestrians are just objects in the way of a COW. As one COW told me, "Don't tell me that people aren't objects, haven't you ever hit one with your car?" Pedestrians never have the right-of-way in today's society.

Tipping the COW: This is a tough one because you don't want your remedies to put you in more of harm's way. One remedy is to whip out that trusty cell phone and pretend to be calling a cop. If the driver acts even stupider, then go ahead and call 911.

It is also effective to keep eye contact with the motorist who is slowly creeping forward to dart in front of you. This eye contact forces the COW to recognize that you are a fellow human with rights and feelings. Lock eyes with them, shake your head, "NO" and take a small step forward. But don't make your expression one that provokes confrontation or aggressiveness with the driver only enough to let the driver know you are on the same planet.

Handicap Spaces

The people who park in handicapped spaces should spend just one week with a real handicap, such as walking an extra ten feet to get into the store. And shopping centers, strip malls, store parking lots should be empowered to give those fifty dollar fines that are menacingly announced on the impotent handicapped parking only sign. Let the store employees enforce these fines and let the stores keep the revenue. Local police don't enforce these violations and we shouldn't expect them to do so. If we expect our police to be cruising the parking lots continuously to pinch handicap violators then other, more serious crimes may run rampant.

Tipping the COW: Municipalities should not only mandate that store security gives these tickets; they should give them incentives to do so. Towns should split the ticket price in half with the stores. You betcha that there would be less people parking in the handicapped spaces. Heck, a store could afford to hire another employee just to wander around the parking lots. They could police the lots, pick up the carts, the litter and make money for the store all in one fell swoop.

I must confess that I do wonder if these ignorant people do have a handicap, that is, they are just too mentally deficient to have procured themselves a handicap sticker for their car. And then there are the politically connected COWs who somehow obtained a handicap sticker. So what? They save a few steps by parking closer. Ever notice that these COWs have the bodies that resemble the basis of this acronym?

And how about those cretins that borrow granny's handicap sticker just so they can get the closest parking space to the store to waddle up and get their giant size BBQ cheese curls and liter of orange soda? They are so smug in thinking they've got the world by the tail. They've pulled the ultimate fast one on everyone else. Do they realize the hardship that a truly handicapped person has to go through while they're king of the world? Not only should these COWs get that newly enforced parking fine, but they should be charged with identity theft as well. Let's see how smug they waddle up to the judge in court.

General Courtesy

You let a person turn into your lane and you don't get a thank you wave. People take advantage of your kindness as if they are entitled to that courtesy.

Tipping the COW: Honk your horn (Yea, I know I said they should be banned. But, hey, as long as they're there.) and give the person a huge hearty wave ala Pee Wee Herman. Hopefully, you will shame at least some of these COWs into correcting the behavior for the next guy.

Driving and Sexism

How about the guys that cackle at girls from their cars, can anyone explain the purpose of that? Do they really believe that by yelling sexist epitaphs and making animal like mouth noises that these girls are going to jump into their rusted out fifteen-year-old car and have wild sex with them? I think not. Has this ever worked? How brain dead can these guys be?

Most young ladies have the correct solution for these Neanderthals. You do not yell back, do not smile, do not give the middle finger salute, or any sign that indicates that you recognize their existence. Any sign of stimulation, positive or negative, and these Cretans have accomplished what they set out to do.

Of course, guys with motorcycles who adjust the mufflers to make louder noise are in this Neanderthal category also. Do these COWs think that girls are going to faint at the sound of their big powerful machine? Well, there are actually a group of girls who may do just that, but these are not the type of girls who you bring home to introduce to mom and dad anyway.

I do wonder if the ancestors of these motorcycle Casanovas tried to attract ladies by stuffing megaphones in their horse's rear ends and hoping they would fart?

Cars as Loudspeakers

What is the mental disability of these people who insist that cars are moving public address systems? They blast their radios as loud as they can.

71

The noise level is offensive, but do they care about the feelings of others? The answer is obvious and the observation is obvious. This is ignorant and disrespectful behavior done with no regard for others. This is one of the most noticeable examples of I-am-the-center-of-the-world behavior.

Tipping the COW: Don't confront the uncivilized. This is precisely why we pay taxes for police. Most communities have ordinances against noise. Remember a license plate and call the police and register a complaint. If everyone took this attitude then the crude noisemakers would be so hassled for their bad manners they would be forced to change their behavior.

There is the inherent satisfaction of knowing that these COWs will be deaf well before they reach middle-age. They may still be playing their music loud, but then it will be because they have to.

Parking

Parking opens up a huge discussion of rude behavior. Why do they even bother to paint lines on the pavement of parking lots? It certainly isn't to help you remember where you parked. 'Where did we park?…um,oh…I remember it was between the yellow lines. No one seems to adhere to any courtesy in parking. COWs who think they have the most precious car on the planet regularly take up two parking spaces for their priceless cars. These COWs think that the yellow lines are just a suggestion. If they didn't paint yellow lines every so often then the parking lots would be an endless boring black.

And shopping carts, what a classic example of COW behavior. The stores can't go more out of their way to provide places for the shopping carts to be placed. They provide cart corrals, they have teenagers collect the carts, and they just about have the carts on electromagnets that automatically return themselves. But the COW couldn't be bothered to walk another few paces to return a shopping cart to the proper place. As a result, shopping carts are left in front of your car and my car so that they will bump into our paint jobs and dent the metal. Somehow the COW has enough energy to get up, drive to the store, get all of their purchases, bring it to the car and put it in, but for some reason they can't push an empty cart 10 feet.

Tipping the COW: Could everyone please say something when they see a COW leave their cart in a parking space. The more they are called accountable for this behavior, the more they may be shamed into walking four more steps to put them in the cart corral.

Tipping the COW: The same security people who give out tickets for those parking in the handicap spaces (And the store gets a percentage of their labors.) could give these COWs a ticket for not putting away their shopping cart. The proceeds of this ticket would go directly to the store to pay for this extra parking lot employee. Heck, the revenue saved from just not losing those carts would pay for the extra employee. Another aspect of this remedy could be that this ticket gets recorded right into the cash register's computer. In most grocery stores everything else is being recorded on these registers anyway. The offender would be identified the next time they shop at that grocery chain. They would either have to pay or at least be embarrassed in the process.

Don't you love it when you are waiting for the only possible parking space in a full lot. You follow and wait for a person to return to their car only to have them take their (and your) sweet time while they primp themselves check their purchases, converse with their passengers, make a phone call, or anything else but get in and back out as a courtesy to you because you were waiting patiently for their spot. So typical of the COW, these drivers are oblivious to what's happening around them.

Tipping the COW: With a big smile toot your horn with some short bursts and with a quizzical expression ask if they are leaving. These COWs will get the message.

Mobile Phones

"If God intended man to talk and drive, he would have given phone booths wheels."

—Ancient proverb

How many people do you know who can walk and chew gum at the same time? Not many, yet if people cannot drive and talk on the phone in the car then why do they attempt this. These COWs make a call or get a call and they slow down their vehicle to dangerous levels to have their conversation. Moreover, they drive outside of their lanes swerving while they chat about some nonessential matter in their life. For such cows we recommend call waiting—WAIT to get off the road before making your CALL.

COWs, please, only use a mobile phone if you can coordinate driving in your usual manner and talking on the phone.

Although this chapter is about transportation, this whole business with mobile phones and other personal technologies has gotten out of hand. COWs have their phones ringing in the rudest places, as well as beepers, watches, and PDA's (Personal Data Assistants, such as Palm Pilots™).

The other Sunday I looked behind me in church after hearing a ringing noise in the pews. When I looked back a gentleman sitting alone was happily plunking away with his stylus at his PDA while the service was going on. Now, fella, why are you even in church if you are going to attend to the PDA more than the minister? Are you that important of a COW that God communicates to you through your PDA? I looked back several times out of curiosity just in the event that this was a momentary lapse, but sure enough each time I looked back there he was with his stylus poking at the little machine. (No, I did not let it spoil my communication with God. I'm sure God understood that I was collecting a story for this book. After all, God is omniscient.) But, perhaps this is too judgmental, after all we were in church and those who throw the first stone, etc. Maybe this guy was just organizing his sins for a later Email to www.redemption.com.

Some people still show at least slight decorum with cell phones in public places. Probably due more to the fact that they don't want their little secrets overheard by everyone in earshot. But, I lay awake at night fearing that cell phones will go the way of pagers. So few people show any civility toward others when it comes to their pagers. These annoying things go off in all sorts of awkward places. And now using all types of different noises from jingles, to show tunes, to boat horns. Some genius thought that infusing these belt ornaments with a variety of sounds may make them less annoying, but the opposite has happened. They are more annoying than ever. I don't welcome hearing the Star Spangled Banner chimed by an electronic device at the climatic moment of a movie. It is even worse if you are in the bathroom, unless you're already standing.

And look at the reaction of the COW when their pager goes off in an inappropriate place. The less mature the COW, the more they sort of giggle and immediately lose their body language expresses an attitude of, 'look how important I am'. Don't these people realize that everyone knows that you're not a brain surgeon or presidential advisor that just has to be contacted right this very minute on a life and death matter. Come on, not since the seventies have people felt that everyone carrying a pager is a doctor or a person of any importance for that matter. Pagers in today's world are more of a toy than a communication device.

In fact, the more important you are the more likely you are harder to get through directly. You're either too busy to be contacted directly or you have other people around you to answer phones. Think about that COWs. You do not impress anyone anymore. Go play with some other toys. Hopefully ones that are not as annoying.

Tipping the COW: Let the management of the theatre you're in, the restaurant you're dining at, or the museum you are visiting, that your time was wasted. If you paid a fee, politely ask for it back. If enough of us do this then possibly public places will establish policies which demand such devices are turned off. Wouldn't it be nice to have an announcement <u>spoken</u>

prior to the start of a play or movie that ordered all such devices turned off?

Trucks

It appears that long gone are the days when truck drivers considered themselves professionals who maintained a standard of excellence in the performance of their duties. Many years ago truck drivers were proud of their profession. They displayed this pride not only in their work, but in how they presented themselves. To have your Teamsters Union pin on your hat or lapel was a statement of who you were. There was a code of conduct that was shared by these drivers.

Today, truck drivers seem unkempt, reckless, and ruthless. Trucks speed in the far left lane when previously this lane was off limits to their rigs. They drive with abandon because they are driven by getting to the destination fast so they can pick up the next load and on and on.

Speed is such an issue with truckers these days that you see evidence of their addiction to speed in the care of their trucks and loads. Loads are not properly tied down and that makes the truck swerve on the road because of the imbalance in weight. Loads are not tarped (covered) properly or at all, causing debris from the load to fly all over the road. As the debris flies, it finds a captive target in the automobiles that are always sandwiched between the caravan of trucks that dominate any US highway. Stones, metal parts, wood, any haul with some substance behind it can become damaging and possibly lethal when it comes flying off an uncovered truck. This happens so frequently that windshield replacement companies are now a multimillion dollar business in the United States and one of the fastest growing segments in the whole auto accessory field. I often wonder if the trucking unions have bought stock in these companies and are trying to increase profits.

Tipping the COW: The problem with remedying this situation is that car damage from trucks not tarped or loads not balanced happens on the go. A rock or other item being shipped flies out of the back of a truck so quickly that there is no time to get the license plate or other information from the truck.

Most states have laws that say that a truck carrying stones and other building materials have to be tarped. But these laws are seldom enforced. There are just too many trucks out there at once for the police to bother with this violation.

What to do? The only remedy is to try and catch up to the truck and copy down their license plate and company name. All commercial trucks have to display their company name and their commerce numbers on the side of the driver's cab. Copy down all numbers and all names on the side (usually) of the truck. Then don't try and be a policeman yourself. Do what a friend did. He was driving down a highway behind a truck carrying gravel. It was a hot summer day and the truck's load was untarped. The wind was brisk and stones were flying out of the back of the truck. He tried to drive as far back as he could drive without getting into a rear end collision, yet the stones still bounced like rubber balls on the hot asphalt and hit his six month old car. The stones left large paint chips all over the hood of the car. Knowing that the damage was already done, my friend sped up and waited until he could pass the truck. He copied down the name of the company and all other identifying information. Then when he arrived at his office, he called information and finally got the name of the trucking company. Much to his surprise the manager of the company took down the time of the incident, the truck information and then told my friend to get his car painted and the company would pay for it, no questions asked. He did just that. He had his entire car painted and it never cost him a cent.

One wonders whether these truck drivers ever drive automobiles. Don't they see when they're behind the wheel of their own auto what rudeness they are inflicting on everyone else? Like so many of the uncivilized behaviors that this book has been pointing out, if the COWs would just take one moment to put themselves in the position of others what a difference it would make.

Air Travel—Passengers

Airline travel has become the cesspool of rude, COW behavior. No longer do passengers consider traveling on an airplane as an event that calls for decorum, respect of other customers, or common sense.

COWs insist on bringing oversized bags as carryon luggage and trying to squeeze these bulging bags into the overhead compartment. As they struggle with their impossible task, they wheeze and puff air as though it is the fault of the aircraft for giving them, the COW, so much trouble. All the while this scene is taking place, a line of people is waiting behind this COW trying to get to their seat.

This scene reminds me of the cartoon where the fat lady tries on shoes many sizes too small insisting that they fit. She sweats and struggles too prove her point just like these travelers who insist that their carryon will fit in the compartment.

Today's air travel is defined by waiting. No one in their right mind can fantasize that their traveling experience will be a race to save time so common on, check your bags. You not getting out of the airport in record setting time. Any one who has cut their time so close that doesn't take into account that air travel will take an agonizing amount of time is foolish, a bad business person or both. What a COW.

Could people please take a bath or shower before they travel on a plane? You are going to sit shoulder-to-shoulder with strangers for hours your body odor will undoubtedly effect the passengers on either side of you. Perhaps the airlines need to add to their preflight announcements, "In the event that you are seated next to a stinky person, an oxygen mask will fall from above your head and a bar of soap will fall on them.

In coach class, how much does a passenger gain by putting their seat back? The answer is little or nothing. Unless their idea of in-flight entertainment is to see someone suffer. But, the effect is very uncomfortable for the passenger behind you. STOP! As much as the airlines are ballyhooing more room on planes, it continues to be an extreme annoyance to have the person in front of you put the seat back.

Tipping the COW: There are several remedies here. One is to mention this rudeness to the passenger in front of you. Of course, this hardly ever works. You are typically greeted with some rude epitaph in return. Such as,

"I paid for my ticket, too." Or some other ingenious comment. Try calling the flight attendant and ask them to ask the other passenger to upright their seat. This works a bit more often because most people have slightly more respect for the airline staff over you.

Better remedy would be for the airlines to make an announcement that pushing the seat backs down will cause the discomfort of the passenger behind you. Please do so only if you feel it is absolutely necessary. Why can't airlines act civilly and make such an announcement? Why not go all the way and weld the seats into a permanent upright position? The extra centimeter of room you get by putting the seat back is really not worth all the aggravation.

Flight attendants deserve special mention here. They herd a lot of COWs through airplanes everyday at a great emotional and physical cost. COWs treat flight attendants as wait staff in the air. Passengers treat flight attendants as if they are there for their every need. Sadly, the airlines and the flight attendants propagate this notion by not orientating the public on the purpose of the flight attendants. As a result, passengers don't really understand the role of the flight attendant. So between the COWs on board and the general ignorance of what flight attendants are supposed to be doing for the passengers, you have an impossible environment to work in.

Tipping the COW: You have plenty of time in the air to make another announcement on the role and duties of your flight attendants on board. Another remedy would be to stop the meal and beverage service on planes. This custom started years ago to make the passengers more comfortable with the experience of flying when flying was in its infancy. Its usefulness

81

has been long outlived. Give me a few bucks off on my ticket and I can do without the gourmet meal (sic) and fizzed out beverage. Have one flight attendant on duty for safety issues only and save the rest of the costs.

Exiting an airplane is an extreme example of COW behavior. So much so that people should moo while they exit. In fact, if people would moo while they exit then maybe they would remind the other passengers of how much they are acting like COWs. So let's everyone moo at those passengers who feel compelled to push themselves out of the plane before the plane even stops at a gate or stand up the minute the plane touches down to grab at their overhead baggage which is oversized and COWish to begin with.

Tipping the COW: Let everyone begin to moo at these COWs while they act so selfish. A moo under one's breath may just change someone's, one person's, behavior or at the very least will possibly make someone think about their crudeness.

Air Travel—Airline Personnel

Could airlines be a bit more honest with the public? If something isn't going the way it should, please communicate with the passengers. Do this both in the air and on the ground. For example, if a flight is late, make an announcement. Make a verbal announcement not just depend on posting the new time on the board and rely on the public to remember to read the board. These boards are not as efficient as a public address announcement.

The smallest commercial aircraft holds 132 passengers yet airport waiting areas have less than 40 seats. There has to be a more efficient design that an architect could develop which will conserve space and accommodate more people. If passengers have to wait in uncomfortable waiting areas particularly with today's long delays, they will be more likely to complain, liter, vandalize, etc. It makes good business sense to make air travel more comfortable, so start the process at the gate while people wait.

Finally, Could the flight crew please let people know what happened after we hit a pocket of turbulence. Most of the time the plane rocks like it hit a bump and the flight crew doesn't say a word of what happened. At a moment like that, just look around at the faces of fellow passengers. They're concerned. The flight crew may be used to this minor air shifts, but many of the passengers are not. Let the passengers know even at the slightest shift in air turbulence. People will feel comfortable and safe.

Cyclists

Bicycles are vehicles under the law. As such they are governed by laws for their use in most areas of the United States. Most people are unaware that there are laws that govern bicycles. These laws are just as enforceable and serious as those written for motor vehicles. Many of the laws that govern bicycles are the same laws that cover the use of motor vehicles. For example, bicycles are supposed to stop at stop lights, but they seldom do.

Probably the most serious COW behavior that cyclists perform is they drive on paths and sidewalks and dart around pedestrians with wild abandon. First, they are supposed to be on streets or marked bicycle paths. Second, they are supposed to let pedestrians and other cyclists know they are coming upon them when they approach from behind. Seldom do you see either of these safety habits being exercised by cyclists.

Tipping the COW: If you are walking down a path and a bicycle passes you from behind let the bike riders know that they should have announced they were coming. A quick phrase such as, "Let me know you're coming," works well.

Car Repairs

We are now officially slaves to auto repair shops. Car engines with their computer chips cannot be touched by the average person. Only a repair shop with the computer interface can diagnose what is wrong with your car. This also means that more and more we are at the mercy of the services of the auto dealer. The small jack-of-all-trades, neighborhood mechanic often cannot afford the computer based diagnostic tools that will properly diagnose your car's ills. This conveys a great deal of power to the car dealer over our property. This power opens up the possibility of abuse. Sadly, the car dealerships have often taken advantage of this power in the relationship with the customer.

Some favorite examples of car dealerships taking advantage of the public are the higher price they bill out their mechanics' labor hours compared to what free standing repair shops charge for a mechanic's time. Shouldn't a car dealership be able and willing to charge less? First, the dealership is making large profits off other things they sell, such as cars and parts. The independent is only selling service. Second, the car dealership is marketing to you every time you walk in for service. One would think that getting you in the door is worth a discount on car repairs. Have you ever priced a major repair like brakes at a car dealer versus taking it to an independent repair shop. You will routinely pay double at the car dealership for the same repair done by union mechanics and using original replacement parts.

Replenishing your windshield washer fluid is another gross example of let the buyer beware. You take your car in for service and routinely they check 'all the fluid levels' as part of this maintenance. The problem is that they charge $2.99 per gallon for windshield wiper fluid that they get for $.39 per gallon and anyone can buy for $.89 per gallon at a grocery store. You could fill up your reservoir with cheap champagne for less. Further, if your car only needs to be 'topped off' and doesn't need a whole gallon, they will charge you as if they used a whole gallon anyway. Like many such little annoyances, who is going to complain about $2.00? And what's the big deal with the $2.50 that the dealer is making at your annoyance? Well, if a dealer works on 50 cars in one day, that $125.00 the dealer makes over this little scam pays the salary of two porters or one mechanic. The bottom line is that the windshield washer fluid should be free.

Speaking of free, how about the phantom free car wash that many dealers brag about when you bring your car in for service? How many times do they make one of the following excuses: A) Forgot. B) Too busy. C) We could do it, but you'll have to wait 30 minutes longer. Or D) We didn't think you wanted it, your car is so clean.

Why offer something that is not going to be delivered? If a car dealership is gouging us on such little expenses such as windshield washer fluid and car washes can we trust them not to be gouging us on larger expenses. A big fat Heffer COW to car dealer's service centers.

Tipping the COW: Always think elsewhere for your car repairs until the car dealers smarten up. Develop a little checklist for yourself based on past experience and then next time you take your car in for repairs recite from your checklist, "…and I don't need my window washer fluid filled…I don't need new wiper blades…etc. etc.

Hotels

The hotel and hospitality industry should be as anti COW as you can get, but there are plenty of examples of COWs in this industry. Right from the start check-in clerks act as if they own the corporation at check-in. Try asking for an upgrade to a reservation. They always try and put you in the sparsest possible room, the broom closet if they could get away with it, when the hotel is 30% full. Does it cost them any less to give you an empty room that may have a better view? More space? Why can't the hotel's attitude be just the opposite, put the guest (A funny word they use to describe us.) in the best unfilled room possible automatically. Wouldn't you just be sucked in to coming back if you once heard a clerk at check-in say, "Madam, you reservation calls for one of our economy rooms, but we have an elegant room with the best view in the hotel not booked for this weekend. I'm going to put you in this upgrade as our guest." After you awake from fainting you realize that the word guest really applies at this establishment. Maybe the hotel could even give you an incentive package that is honest and fair. Eat at our restaurant for one of your meals each day and the hotel will give you an upgraded room. Hotel restaurants are notorious white elephants for the hotel's bottom line so the hotel gives you something they are not going to sell anyway, the unused upgraded room, <u>and</u> they make more money off you than they were going to if you didn't get this little courtesy. Everyone is happy and everyone feels as if they are treated civilly.

Instead, most of the time the reception clerk treats you at best as if you are a nuisance, and at worst as if they are constipated and it's your fault. What do hotels that are not fully booked do with the better rooms? Are they waiting for Prince Andrew and the London party boys to arrive out of nowhere? Do they reserve them for family and friends to use gratis? At the very least, there should be a Solomonesque approach at the front desk. "Yes, I can upgrade you for a very slight charge."

Hotel Shuttles

Do these vehicles really operate? They seem to just sit out in front of the hotel like decorations. Try asking the hotel staff if that car can take you to the airport and you typically get back, "We don't have shuttle service." THEN WHY IS THE VEHICLE SITTING OUT FRONT OF THE HOTEL?

<u>**Tipping the COW:**</u> Wouldn't it be nice if the hotel would actually use the vehicle? This civil behavior goes a long way toward customer satisfaction and repeat business. Although am I sure, that same efficiency expert that all these businesses seem to borrow has the gas expenditure and

staff time lost calculated down to the mili-cent if this vehicle moves off the grounds.

Concierges

Hotels, please don't put up these nameplates advertising a concierge service unless it really exists. Recently I checked in at an upper tier hotel and then walked over to the unattended 'concierge' desk. I waited for service only to find that the young person who just checked me in, and did so rather curtly, just shuffle stepped over to perform that duty also. Now as the concierge he donned a smile. Do hotels think we are stupid? Now, that's COW behavior.

OK, so the hotel does have a concierge and they are professional in their presentation. The whole point of being a concierge is to have an opinion. Yet, most concierges appear to have gone to the same schools that train shrinks. They talk with uncertainty and vagueness. How many times do you hear from these people, "Well, if you're looking for Italian, this place is good, but so is this and this and this and maybe this and even this..." You end up with 16 choices and no opinion if one is better than the other. Instead of showing enthusiasm for a recommendation they surround their recommendations with qualifiers. Or when asked for a recommendation they simply look at the local free pamphlet distributed around the hotel. Please stop being a COW, we can read, we approach concierges because we want a human being to offer an opinion, to take a stand. What's the point?

Hotel Amenities

It wasn't too long ago that hotels began the practice of placing coffee makers in every room. Wasn't that a special touch? On paper it must have seemed like a marketing brainstorm. Can't you just picture the meeting at boardroom of the exclusive hotel chain when the junior associate assistant of marketing helpful strategies proposed putting *Mr. Coffee* pots in every room. Can't you just picture that he or she spiced up this presentation to the board by having a zesty cup of fresh brewed Kona coffee sitting there for each of those in attendance of that person's big moment in the sun? Can't you just hear the thunder of the presentation on how the hotel will corner the market by this simple idea for customer satisfaction and convenience?

Back to reality. When was the last time you used the coffee provided with those cute little mini-coffee makers? Its horrid! So what's happened? They've taken a good idea and ruined it. Yep, the same guy they all share, who knows how to squeeze a penny out of the crevices of the wall, has directed the company to buy cheaper and cheaper coffee to supply those little makers with, so the coffee is undrinkable.

Along with the coffee that no one uses because it is so undrinkable, consider those toiletries that are provided as conveniences. Body lotion is always a standard item, but have you ever tried to use it? The body lotion has as much moisturizing power as lighter fluid. The Q-tips that they provide should come with a warning, "Do not place these inside of your ears as they will fall apart and become lost." These sticks with cotton on them are so flimsy that instead of gently swabbing your ear they scratch it.

89

You must applaud the effort the hotels put into the bottles of mouthwash. A full-time hotel employee must be assigned to intercept each shipment of mouthwash they buy, open each little bottle and carefully remove 96% of the mouthwash and dilute the remaining liquid with water, and seal them back up.

Here's another hotel room tip. Skip the chalk dust paste that they pass off as toothpaste, and rub your toothbrush on the bar soap they provide. Use this as your toothpaste, it's tastier and cleans better.

Tipping the COW: Hotels, please remove the coffee pot, shampoo, mouthwash, body lotion, toothpaste and whatever else, we'll bring our own, and take $10.00 per night off my room charge. Let's all ask for this each time we check into a hotel and see what happens.

Chapter Seven
Conversation...

Do please and thank you just not exist anymore? I don't know where they went, but, poof, they disappeared right out of the English language. If you want to visit them they reside in dictionaries, like sitting in a museum. Like many museum exhibits they are not alive in the real world. We don't request people to do things, we order them to or we grunt at them and expect them to translate our wishes.

We do not approach people with dignity and kindness; sadly, we approach them in a manner that we believe will get what we want.

Tipping the COW: We have to stop responding to people who don't request things from us in a civil manner.

Yelling, loudness, rudeness, foul language have all deteriorated beyond belief. People have gotten the message that yelling at someone gets their attention, makes them behave differently or expresses one's authority over another. None of this is true of course. In fact, yelling always accomplishes the opposite. Just think about your boss confronting you about a mistake. If he or she approaches you steaming and yelling, the first thought you have in your head is, "I'll just wait this out and go on and do my business as I always have." And that is precisely what you do. You mentally turn off the yelling and you return to your work doing exactly how you did it prior to the confrontation. This is human nature. We automatically turn off yelling and hostility.

<u>Tipping the COW:</u> Real power in relationships comes from establishing respect from others. Not from using foul language, yelling or being otherwise abusive. We establish respect by being firm, businesslike, proving our points to the other person with facts and information, and by having firm, effective consequences for the other person that we are going to consistently and powerfully inact on the other person.

Being able to establish consequences and gaining respect when we converse with others not only works well in adult-to-adult relationships, but also is poignantly true in parent-to-child relationships. The minute we allow yelling to enter our relationship with our children (from age 3 to 33) we have lost whatever result we were trying to achieve. Think about it. If my six year old calls me "the worst parent in the world" because I make them eat their beans at the dinner table should I get myself emotionally distraught and feel guilty because my child just said I'm the worst parent in the world? Of course not. We dismiss this rant of the six year old and have the confidence that we know we are making the right choice for our child. What is the emotional difference between that scenario and the eighteen year old calling me the worst parent in the world, and using the 'F' word, because I won't let them drink beer with the other teenagers? There <u>is</u> no difference between these two children. They both represent childish temper tantrums. Only the eighteen-year-old's actions and language appears to be more threatening. You should react to the nonsense that an eighteen year-old brings to you just as you did when that child was six years-old.

Sixteen year old immature child, "Hey, F…king dad, I want some beer with my dinner." Dad, "All right, you can have your beer, but finish your beans first."

Tipping the Cow: In situations when you or someone else is about to yell, use the Railroad (RR) technique. If you are about to yell at your kids <u>or</u> you are about to be yelled at by someone, just picture a bright red railroad crossing sign in your mind. The two R's should stand for: R = don't respond and R = don't reinforce. The first R' should represent the best way to stop yelling. If you don't respond, then the yelling will stop. Too many yelling matches escalate because neither party just stops the yelling. To stop yelling in its tracks (sic) you can also use the physical technique of crisscrossing your index fingers on each hand to resemble a railroad crossing sign. When a family member starts yelling, put up your hands in this manner. It works just like a 'time out' sign. The RR sign let's everybody know you're done talking as soon as the voices are raised and the yelling/arguing starts.

Now, the other person may still want to yell and argue even though you've expressed to them that you will not participate in a conversation that is offensive. In this case, the next step is to leave, yes, leave. Why, you may ask, should I leave? Why, for two reasons. First, it definitively stops the offensive conversation. Second, if you want to train the other person that you <u>really</u> will not tolerate or reinforce yelling or any offensive conversation, then leaving is the best method to do this. You gain nothing by staying in these conversations and trying to yell over someone. (Especially your family members.) Sure you can do it, but what have you taught them except that there will be another one of these yelling conversations soon.

Leaving the scene is a form of the second R. If you leave the scene you don't reinforce the yelling. Shouldn't the yelling child be given consequences for such behavior? Sure, but that should come later after you have deescalated the situation and regained control. That's when you can apply consequences. And what consequences to apply is the topic of another book.

The RR technique can be used for any COWish behavior but it works so well for language you just do not want to hear. Use it liberally when you hear the F… word. Let's try to extinguish the F… word.

Speaking of the 'F' word, our language has become increasingly punctuated with profanity. No longer contained to pubescent locker rooms, profanity has entered into every type and setting of conversation. It has become acceptable to use profane language in places that were shocking only ten years ago. This language invasion is highlighted not to call for a blanket of censorship to cover conversations, but to point out how impotent it is to use profanity. The use of profanity in conversations is such a clear example of how little power uncivil behavior contains and conversely how powerful civil behavior is.

Think of how easy it is to pull a profanity out of the air and apply it at will in a conversation. Now, try and replace the profanity with a substitute word or words that are just as powerful. What you will find is that, in fact, these new words will get another person's attention much more effectively than the profanity. Unless, of course, the other person is an intercoursing idiot.

Interestingly, just like the universal signal of the raised middle finger, profanity has lost its power to shock or to even punctuate a conversation. With overuse, profanity has lost its power.

Language has lost its power as well. Currently, there is a raging debate on the value of the S.A.T. tests as a measure of college acceptance. The knowledgeable opponents of the S.A.T. argue that low income students are not surrounded by the language skill acquisition that their middle and upper-middle income counterparts are exposed to from early childhood onward. Because they start life with weaker language skill development lower income students are postulated to do poorer on such standardized tests s the S.A.T. and the A.C.T. Both of these tests stress language skills and the test taker does appreciably better if they have greater language skills. Quite an argument for increasing the power of language, heh?

If we would extend this argument and examine the components of the language in common usage it becomes alarming to discover that the distillation of the power of language is happening in all segments of our society. Yes, lower income communities are still leading the way in surrounding their children with powerless language, but the middle and upper classes are catching up quickly. So civility, here by using more powerful, civil language, has its inherent rewards. It increases power, respect and success.

One uncivilized behavior that has a great deal of power in conversation is lying. Like so many of the uncivilized behaviors discussed in this book, lying has invaded society and has attached itself to our relationships like a blood sucking leach. Presidents lie, the government lies, parents lie, police lie, everyone seems to lie. Lying undercuts the conversations we engage in by ways that cannot be corrected. The biggest problem with lying is that no matter how skilled one is in relationships or conversations, no one can detect liars for certain.

Tipping the COW: Lying should be treated as one of the most heinous of crimes. Do not let lying go unpunished. In children, make a big deal of correcting lying at an early age and you will prevent this behavior from escalating as your children grow.

Listen to the conversations of COWs. They talk about themselves and their lives with little interest in others. Conversation usually implies that two people are involved but when a COW is involved you can bet the conversation is one sided. They discuss their day, what they had for lunch or how their day went. Interject some of your concerns and you get the classic, "Oh…OK…well as I was saying,". Your words are just not as important as theirs and they take it as their duty to teach us poor bastards how to live no matter how successful or how long we have walked this earth.

Tipping the COW: Teach the other person how you want to have a conversation. Sounds unusual but we actually do this all the time but we do it subliminally. It happens when we perk up, give added attention, and show facial expression when another person begins to talk about a subject we are most interested in. You can also make this a very conscious process by noting how you want to converse. For example in a conversation with someone that talks too much, add phrases to the conversation such as, "Is it my turn yet?" or "Hey, I've got something to say about that." or "Can I say something now?" If these people don't get the idea, then take a stronger tactic by saying something like, "You know I don't always enjoy our conversations because I can't get a word in edgewise." These phrases and other actions you take are really teaching tools that will teach the other person how to have a civil conversation. When you act like this toward someone else you are not being rude or disrespectful you are being a teacher of civil behavior.

Chapter Eight
In Relationships…

The utmost civility in relationships is to continually be honest. More people get into relationship problems because they are not honest with others. Often people are not honest with each other not because they want to be evil but because they feel the truth will hurt the other's feelings. People mistake this for being a form of helping the other person. It is actually uncivil behavior to lie in order to avoid hurting someone's feelings. The addictions specialists call these lies, enabling.

One cannot have a relationship with a lie. A lie represents something that does not exist. It may be an action that was or was not done, feelings that do or do not exist, or anything else that one may fabricate, but it does not exist in reality by definition. If you were going sky-diving you would not want the instructor to 'not hurt your feelings' by not telling you that you have a bad parachute.

A good example of uncivil behavior is how people end relationships with each other. When people are trying to end a relationship they often go through this period where they are not honest about their feelings and desires. What they want to say is that they don't want to see the other person again, but what they end up saying is, "Ok, I'll have lunch with you." Or some other variation on the little lie that doesn't convey their true feelings. How is this helping the other person when you lie about this? In civil relationships, people are honest with each other and express their true desires in an upfront manner.

This lack of civility toward each other is also dramatically evident in relationships when a person must deal with another who has problems. There is some mythical thinking that one is being a 'good friend', 'helping', or 'forgiving' to another when they enable the person to continue their dysfunctional behavior. We give alcoholics that next drink, we excuse foul language as just the way he or she is, and we ignore violent outbursts as a 'temper problem'.

Tipping the COW: Civil behavior is to not forgive negative behavior in others. Acting civilly is helping to correct negative behaviors by teaching the offender to change by not enabling negative behaviors.

Youth are the biggest offenders of this relationship toward others. In fact, if one reads into these school shooting incidents of recent years you discover that in almost each case, the teen offenders have talked to peers about their intentions. But, whether trying to be better pals or some other motivation, the peer group did not make efforts to stop the violent teens.

Tipping the COW: It is wrong to accept other's negative behavior and our children need to be taught that this is not helping a friend. True help takes into consideration the future of the person and the ultimate consequences if the person doesn't stop their friend. Parents need to pay close attention to teach their children this vital lesson of friendship and helping others. Go out of your way to make sure you understand this and can convey it to your children.

Listening

Listening is a lost art in today's society. Whether it is the supersonic pace of modern life or just a general lack of caring, but no one listens any longer. Shrinks and pseudo shrinks are paid good money to listen to others. In fact, if one wonders how these self-proclaimed therapists can proliferate in the face of better trained psychologists, psychiatrists, and social workers, it is because it doesn't take years of training in graduate schools to simply smile and listen to someone.

Listening is an active process and is not just being silent while another talks. Listening requires understanding what the person is communicating and having empathy for their statements. Listening also requires the listener to convey this understanding and empathy for the conversation they are hearing.

Tipping the COW: How do you learn how to be a better listener? Try these exercises when in a conversation with someone. First, as the person is talking repeat this mantra to yourself, "What are they describing?" say this over and over while the other person is talking. Second, use your imagination. As the person is talking say to yourself, "Can I picture what they are talking about?" Then as they talk, try to paint a picture in your mind of what they are describing. If you can't create a picture in your mind, then ask questions that will help you paint that picture. Ask questions that help you paint this mind portrait of what the other person is talking about. Asking questions is not interrupting or blocking the conversation if they are focused on the other person's messages. Third, be empathetic to the conversation of the other person. Being empathetic requires you to ask yourself, "How did that feel?" continuously while the other person describes something.

Being a good listener to others is an outstanding way to treat others with the highest degree of civility. It is how we connect as humans. More than anything people want to be heard as individuals. Most often people are not looking for advice but to know that someone else understands what they are going through.

Defining

Defining is an excellent tool in relationships. People take for granted what they are communicating is understood by the other person. Never take for granted that the other person knows what you are speaking about particularly when you are using emotionally charged words. I'm sad, I'm mad, I'm depressed, he's bad, or other such phrases may mean one thing to you, but may mean something entirely different to the person you are communicating with.

Tipping the COW: Always check whether the other person has a definition of what you are trying to communicate. Never take it for granted that the other person has this definition just because you speak the same language.

Relationship with Relatives

Brothers, sisters and other relatives have a particularly difficult time treating each other civilly. Ever notice how strangers always get better treatment from your siblings than you do? There is some logic to this practice. After all you don't pick your relatives and siblings but you do choose who your friends will be. So, if your sibling or relative acts like a COW, you have no obligation to put up with that behavior. Some people feel that the rude behavior of a sibling or relative should be tolerated just because this is a relative. In fact, tolerating uncivilized behavior in such people just supports their rude, COW like behavior and allows or enables them to continue to do this to others. Supporting this behavior is not good for you and it is not good for them.

Funny, when we encounter a little bug in our homes, we tend to smash it, as if to say, 'let this be a lesson to all you other bugs.' Yet, if someone comes over and insults us we just smile. I bet that if we smiled at the bugs and smacked our relatives, the bug problem would be about the same, but our relatives would treat us better. There should be NO PEST STRIPS for humans. You just put it at your front door and all the nasty people would get stuck to it. "Hey Uncle Bob, stop squirming. As soon as you act right I'll let you in.

Tipping the COW: Change this behavior in relatives and siblings by not accepting it, not feeding into it, and confront it when it is displayed toward you. For example, a friend has a sister who since her divorce has become a bitter person. She is loud and obnoxious in public. Often she colors her language with the most vial of language. She doesn't take care about her appearance so she looks disheveled and dirty. The sister loves to go out with my friend for night life, but she is embarrassing to my friend. For months this went on until my friend couldn't take anymore. Going out with her lewd sister gave her panic attacks. She asked for my advice and I told her to confront her sister about her behavior and tell her that she wouldn't go out with her anymore as long as she continued to act and look this way. I told her to do so is an act of kindness. It is not being mean or insensitive to the situation of her sister. My friend took the advice and confronted her sister. Initially her sister was offended, but after a short period of pouting the sister controlled her tongue and started to take more care with her appearance. They are now back to going out together for night life and they better enjoy each other's company. My friend did the civil thing for her sister and it benefited both of them.

Immaturity

Immaturity is a huge problem in relationships. Immaturity is a huge problem in our society. Whether it is because the younger generation has not suffered through a war, depression, or the constant threat from a foreign power, the fact remains that the younger generation is churning out immature people at an alarming rate. In mental health care of youth, if the vast majority of problems that end up in shrink's offices were properly diagnosed, that diagnosis would be immaturity. The actions of youth such as running away, swearing, curfew violations, and smoking, drinking, minor drug experimentation are the acts of childish youth. They are irresponsible and with the aim of instant gratification. This is the very definition of immature behavior.

Immature people are definitely COWs. The immature person only thinks of their own gratification. Just think of how gratification orientated are young children. Their survival depends on them getting their needs met. Only with maturity does the person develop such characteristics as responsibility, social conscience, and altruism.

Tipping the COW: The remedy for this is to treat the individual according to their maturity level. Not their chronological age level, but by the maturity level they exhibit. This common sense approach can be summed up by the phrase, "Act like a Child, get treated like a Child. Act like an Adult, get treated like an Adult." By treating people in this fashion you accomplish two things. First, you are better emotionally prepared to cope with the other person's behavior. Second, you are correcting the immature behavior of the other person.

Teenagers provide the best vignettes to illustrate this remedy but keep in mind that people of all ages can display immature behavior. An excellent example is when the teenager is not responsible enough to take out the garbage for his parents on a daily basis, but then in the same evening will demand the family car to go over to a girlfriend's house for some adult-like romance. My response to this dichotomy would be to deny the teen the car keys because if he is not responsible enough to take out 2lbs of garbage, he/she certainly is not responsible enough to care for a 2,000 pound, $15,000 family investment such as a car.

Remember, act like a child, and get treated like a child.

Conversely, (Teenagers reading this book pay attention. Snip out this page and highlight it with a yellow highlighter.) if a young person shows responsibility in the majority of their life, gets good grades, is obedient, pleasant around the house, then they should be allowed greater freedoms.

Act like an adult, get treated like an adult.

Dating

Dating relationships should follow the same common sense approach as: Act like an adult get treated like an adult~Act like a child get treated like a child. A similar simple rule should dominate meeting someone and dating. This rule can be stated as:

IF ITS NOT FUN, YOU'RE DONE!

Way too many people force themselves into dating situations that are filled with problems. They find someone with a semi-truck full of baggage and try to make the relationship work. And even if your name is Ima Porter, you are not responsible for carrying other's unresolved baggage. Dating should not be about making it work. Dating should be about having fun and two people making each other feel good. Not necessarily physically feel good, but just having fun, enjoying each other's company, and doing things both of them like to do.

In dating people often concentrate on the wrong agendas. They become lost in the physical attractiveness of the other person, or their sexuality, or their money or power. When they become lost in any one of these agendas they often forget about the fun. The relationship becomes one filled with long discussions about inner turmoil. And the activity in the relationship becomes dominated by one of the couple bailing the other out of the latest inner turmoil.

Tipping the COW: If you see yourself dating someone and all your doing is bailing them out of one situation after another the only bailing you should do is to bail yourself out of that relationship. Do this no matter how beautiful the other is or how sexy they are. Or as the street philosophers say, 'If they are good looking but act like a bitch, it's time for the Bitch Pitch' and 'If they are good looking but suck, they get the You Suck Chuck.'

To adhere to this motto of, 'If it's not fun, you're done' does presuppose that one shouldn't bring their own baggage into a new relationship. This is the civilized thing to do. Don't seek to enter into a new relationship until you have your act together and you can be a giving, fun partner for another. Having your own baggage under control before you date is as important as good grooming. The civil thing to do is to have your baggage under control as one of your pre-dating preparations. A COW grazes out in the dating

106

field when they have all kinds of their own demons that they haven't put to rest. This is like having a social disease and having no conscience about spreading it to others.

Voice Mail/Answering Machines

Voice mail/answering machines are a double edged sword when it comes to the COW syndrome. They can help you to be civilized or uncivilized.

Voice mail has replaced face-to-face confrontation with another. Instead of letting someone know your true feelings by telling them in person, now people leave voice mails. How uncivilized is that? If you are going to break up with someone or need to make some other difficult statement, the civil act would be to tell them to their face or at the very least by a live phone conversation.

Tipping the COW: Before leaving that voice mail message, put yourself in the other person's place. Would you like to hear this news by listening to a message?

On the other hand, voice mail and answering machines have allowed some people to say what they feel when otherwise they would have avoided telling the other person. This impersonal piece of technology makes for a nice defense mechanism that allows one to speak their mind when otherwise they couldn't.

Tipping the COW: The advice here is to do this only in times when you would otherwise avoid speaking altogether. As stated above, always put yourself in the place of the other and think of how you would like to hear this statement.

RING…RING…RING…"Hi, this is Pat, I'm not home right now so please break up with me after the tone."

Isn't it ironic that so many of our outgoing messages on our voice mails and answering machines state some variation of, "Leave a message and I'll return your call as soon as I can."

The problem here is that people have no intention of returning your call. (This is particularly true in California. For some reason Californians just don't call back. Too busy fending off earthquakes, dodging kooks, attending 12 step meetings, or attending to some other personal enlightenment, I guess.) Civil behavior would call for more honesty in our outgoing messages. They would sound something like this: "I'm not here, so keep calling back until you catch me live because I ignore all messages left on this machine."

Privacy

Privacy is an important, civil aspect of close relationships. Just because you are in an intimate relationship with another doesn't mean that you cannot and should not also maintain some privacy for yourself. In fact, couples that have the most serious problems often find that these problems arise because they haven't discovered this need for privacy. Relationships that don't respect this need for each person's privacy end up smothering the other person in the relationship.

Tipping the COW: Do not be guilty about having a private life. It is important and healthy in relationships.

Parents pay attention, teenagers need privacy more at this stage of a person's life than at many other times in their life. Many of the conflicts between parents and teens stem from parents not respecting the teen's privacy. Privacy helps teens learn about independence and identity. It is normal and expected for teens to crave privacy.

Tipping the COW: Parents need to back off on this issue.

In general not respecting other's privacy is a COW thing to do. Think about it, COWs need to know everything about the people they are in relationships with because a COW needs to be the center of the world. Cows cannot tolerate others having a private life without them. Don't be a cow about privacy.

"Son, remember that your mother and I had you not because we wanted to bring a new life into this world, but because we needed more people around for us to tell them what to do."

Chapter Nine
In Sex…

Selfishness in Sex

A common ingredient in sexual dysfunction is selfishness on the part of lovers. Sexuality, because of the intense emotions and gratification involved is by definition an indulgent experience. It is easy to be consumed by selfishness in sex. A common concern of lovers is how they are going to get self satisfied without focusing on how to please the other. Sounds exactly like the characteristics of the COW.

Tipping the COW: The paradox here is that lovers don't realize that the more one concentrates on pleasing the other person the more one will achieve ecstasy for themselves. This is an absolute fact of sexual function. You see, as one obsesses about their own pleasure, the more they can become plagued by performance anxiety. If you concentrate on pleasing the other, your gratification is guaranteed. And the delightful side effect here is that you will become an exquisite lover.

Loss of Sexual Interest

Another common sexual dysfunction is the loss of sexual interest by a partner. Typically, the loss of sexual interest arises out of one of two sources. The first is the loss of interest in one's partner. The second is the interference caused by one's mind being consumed by worries, problems, work, or other concerns. Considering the source of this problem one could easily see how COW's are more susceptible to suffering this problem than others.

For a COW sex is not sharing, not making love, not intimacy, not a physical expression of your love for another person. For a COW, sex is just a physical act that has the goal of their own physical satisfaction. A COW could easily lose interest in their sexual partner because of their narcissistic approach to sex. Their sexual partner could become boring to them, another potential partner may become more attractive, or the act of love making may not be as fulfilling to them with this partner. A COW responds to this loss of sexual interest by giving up and possibly moving to another in the hope that this new person brings more satisfaction to the sexuality.

Tipping the COW: A more noble approach would be to concentrate on working with your partner and making your sex life more fulfilling. There are a variety of methods one can use to work on your sex life together with your partner. This work together in itself can be fulfilling and fun.

111

Machismo

Ever hear a group of male COWs talk about the opposite sex? They concentrate on their satisfaction and treat women as objects. They focus on their body parts and sexualize women's bodies. Unfortunately, these crude men are tolerated by society and because of peer pressure other young men get caught up in behaving like these COWs. It becomes a cycle that has been going on for generations.

Tipping the COW: How do we end this cycle? Men have to speak up when they hear other men talk about women in a depreciating manner. Don't just go along with the 'locker room' talk. At the very least just be silent when these morons talk about sex as if it was about forcing themselves on a woman.

Go out of your way to comment on these COWs who talk about women in a depreciating manner when young people are around. Whether these young people are your children or not don't just let this COWish behavior and statements just hang in the air without a corrective statement. If we don't start doing this then young people will think that it is OK to talk about women this way.

Sex as a Tool

Both sexes use sex as a tool in relationships. To do so is a very COW thing to do. A common tool men use is to put contingencies on sex. These may sound like, 'if you don't give me sex, then I won't give you money' or 'I'm not going to this event unless you come across' or some variation on this male theme song. Now, men, stop and listen to how you sound when you make this COW sound. Do you really get fulfillment when sex is performed under these circumstances? What does this say about you when you have to get sex under these conditions?

Women play their own sexual games. A typical one is withholding sex as a weapon against men. What women don't realize is that by doing this they just perpetuate the cycle of men using sex back against them. So now we have both parties on the sexual teeter-tauter. When one goes up, the other goes down. The very nature of sex becomes distorted in this relationship.

Tipping the COW: Sex isn't about getting an advantage over another. The best sex comes with sharing otherwise its just mutual masturbation. If you want the best sex ever then make sharing your goal, not getting off. Both men and women need to stop reinforcing (providing sex acts) behavior that uses sex as a tool.

Sex and Attractiveness

Like these uncivilized games, couples have other COW habits that sabotage sex for each other. A common dynamic that is never discussed is attractiveness in sex. For a woman, there are many ways in which she can adorn herself to make herself sexually attractive to a man. A multi-billion dollar beauty and clothing industry aggressively supports women to be sex objects. How can any man come close to the amount of assistance that a woman has at her disposal to make herself more attractive to a man she is interested in. It is almost uncivilized (Except we men enjoy it so much and anything you enjoy that much cannot be that uncivilized.) how powerfully alluring any woman can become with all the tools at her disposal. But, ladies, please don't stop!

Men are not impotent in this regard either. (Please excuse the pun. No, wait, I purposely wrote that pun in right here.) But, men seem to abdicate any effort here in adorning themselves. What COWs! Many men don't think that there are steps they can take to make themselves more sexually attractive. Men don't have the same multi-billion dollar industry supporting their sexuality as do women. Sadly, the male sexual attractiveness industry is more silly than effective. Men have at their disposal underwear with elephant trunks or peek-a-boo holes cut out. Women have Victoria Secrets™ and Fredericks™ in comparison. This is not equality of the sexes.

Tipping the COW: But men can do something to enhance their attractiveness and some of the things they can do are the little things that men have forgotten. But, the civilized man who is concentrating on pleasing a partner does these little things. Simple things that men forget that make them more desirable include: TAKE A SHOWER!, use cologne, be well-groomed, and keep your body fit. AND BE ROMANTIC IN SEX!

Chapter Ten
In the Media…

The media can be penultimate COWs. People who work in the media carry themselves with an aplomb as if they are doing the most noble work on the planet. In actuality they are selling products just like the carnival barkers and snake oil salesmen of the late eighteen hundreds. Don't believe that, just study the commercials. Ironically, lotions, medicines, household products and foods are the dominant subjects of the commercials that the media broadcast.

The most obvious loss of civility in the media is the lack of objectivity that exists while the media prides in portraying itself as the paragon of objectivity and fairness. There is no question that the media present messages from the perspective that they want to express to the public. Yet, they portray themselves as objective and presenting both sides of issues. In this way they treat the public in a pejorative manner, as if we don't know that they are doing this thinly veiled rouse. The public is the mark and the sale is the thing in the media. The media is one huge COW.

Tipping the COW: The media has a love/hate relationship with feedback. They invite it, but by the same token they hate it when it is negative. We can help to change the media by writing in to the stations with our comments. Then, copy your letter and send it to the sponsors of the shows. In the media there is strength in numbers, so when you write try and get the signatures of as many friends as possible who agree and support your position. If we do this often enough, then the media will pay attention. Remember, the media is about the sale and we control the sale.

Let's stop the pretense and tell it like it is in the media. News readers feel compelled to call themselves 'journalists' and weather reporters are billed as meteorologists. The public knows full well that they are in front of the camera because they look good. Treat the public with civility and give these pleasant people their correct title: "And reading the news tonight is….. And now reading the weather report is………."

Tipping the COW: To put truth in advertising into the media, a warning should be required to be read that would go something like this:

Warning, this newscast is our interpretation and filtration of the events around you. It is geared toward increasing viewer ship and does not necessarily represent the broad spectrum of events in your community and your world. We have left out many of the frequent acts of civility and kindness that occur everyday in order to present to you the more sensational and unusual events that will grab your attention.

Chapter Eleven
In Restaurants...

Restaurants are public places where one pays for a form of entertainment. They are not personal kitchens and dining rooms that you borrow for a time. The next person is waiting for a chance to pay for their entertainment as well. This is a fundamental philosophy that is very important to civil behavior in restaurants.

As places of entertainment, civil behavior in such entertainment venues calls for consideration for the other people enjoying the entertainment. One of the frequent COW like behaviors seen at restaurants are the people who luxuriate at their table when there is a line out the door of people waiting to get in? These COWs have finished their meal, enjoyed themselves but they are oblivious to the other people who want a turn at enjoying the entertainment they just experienced. Civil behavior would dictate that the finished diners would efficiently move on for the evening.

Tipping the COW: More restaurants should politely and discretely ask finished diners to move out of their table. This treats all customers in a civil manner. Don't restaurants understand that they are setting up a negative attitude with the party waiting even before these people partake in the services? Restaurants should realize it is more in their interest to move COWs along.

Loudness

With the rise of celebrity chefs and restaurants as spectacles of decorations and attractions and with the cost of going to an above average restaurant, dining out has become an evening's entertainment in and of itself. Loud obnoxious behavior by patrons is particularly unacceptable because this is <u>your</u> evening's entertainment. But, loud and obnoxious behavior should be unacceptable no matter what the style of the restaurant.

Tipping the COW: Solution, take a complaint to the staff and insist that they quiet the loud mouth. Not enough restaurants control their crowds. Do not yell at the fellow customer, insult them, and shoot them dirty looks or other such uncivilized behavior on your part. It is guaranteed that these actions in response will just inflame the loud mouth more. Further, it will ruin your time so why do it. You're paying for a dining out experience so that's what the staff is for. If the staff is unresponsive, don't pay for your meal.

Movie Theatres

You should carry this same attitude into the **movie theatre**. It is no secret that the uncivilized hordes crowd into movie theatres and bring their beepers, cell phones and obnoxious behavior with them.

Tipping the COW: Don't confront the COW, find a theatre employee, preferably one that is over fourteen years old, complain and demand your money back and the COW reprimanded. If you don't get satisfaction make sure you contact the ownership of the theatre. That's usually someone over the age of fourteen.

Paying the Bill

How uncivilized is the treatment one receives when your credit card is rejected. A friend of mine had the following experience one Christmas Eve while taking out his family including his aging mother. At the end of an excellent dinner at a fine dining restaurant on the top of a well-known building, the waiter presented the bill. My friend presented a credit card with absolute confidence. As his bill was being processed, at a reception stand in the center of the dining room, the Matre D' and the Captain noticeably pointed out my friend, embarrassingly, with a look of disdain on their faces. After the waiter returned and loudly explained that the credit card was rejected, my friend immediately went to the first floor of the building to a cash station machine and used the same credit card, took out more than enough money for the bill and paid cash for the check and a

119

handsome tip. He presented it directly to the Matre D' politely informing them that this cash was drawn from the same card. None of the restaurant people apologized or acknowledged any possible mistake. Instead they all kept their condescending glare.

Tipping the COW: Needless to say, my friend never patronized that restaurant again. That is the tip one should always employ in this type of situation along with a letter to the restaurant and a copy sent to the local newspaper.

Reception

Speaking of restaurant staff, how rude is it to arrive at a restaurant that has a healthy crowd and as you approach the hostess stand there are six people standing around. They take your name and announce that the wait is ten minutes. Then you are handed a beeper or some other vibrating device that lights up like a cheap Carnival souvenir when your table is ready. The whole time you're standing six feet away from this cabal. When your table is ready not one of them can do the polite, civilized act of approaching you and letting you know your table is ready. Instead they depend on this toyish gizmo to summon you to their command station. Ten minutes, six staff members and six feet away and not one can politely come to you and escort you to a table. To do so may violate some sacred corporate memo that orders them to use the carnival toy instead of the personal touch. Or in ten minutes have they all forgotten who you are and that you are waiting for a table?

What the corporate geniuses are missing is how this attitude sets up the remainder of your experience for that night. Impersonal experience translates to less food and drink purchased, less tipping and less returns.

What about the wait in restaurants in general? How does anyone justify a two hour wait to eat food?

Tipping the COW: There are plenty of restaurants in your area. Don't wait and reinforce these wait times by staying any longer than twenty minutes. If we all do this we will end the reinforcement of these uncomfortable experiences. Go to a smaller restaurant where there is no wait. And be experimental, sure you have come to like a certain place, but if there is a huge wait, try some place new. Part of the fun of dining out is the uniqueness of the food and setting being different from home. Trying a new place just extends this uniqueness one step farther.

Staff Attitudes

The more trendy the restaurant the worse the staff's attitude seems to be. At the popular restaurants the staff attitude seems to reflect an orientation that they are doing the customers a favor by waiting on them rather than the reality that the customers are favoring the restaurant with their patronage.

Tipping the COW: There are several remedies at your disposal. One is to say something to these staff people. Another is to reflect your displeasure in the tip you leave. If you do this, make sure you write a little note on the receipt that explains why you are shorting the tip. People leave small tips as a sign of displeasure, but seldom do they communicate why they are doing so. If you don't communicate the nature of your act, how can the restaurant staff change. There is nothing wrong with shorting the tip like this. Many people feel you are punishing the wait staff for the faults of the Matre D', bus boy or reception staff, but at most restaurants the staff has a custom of pooling the tip so this act is very appropriate and fair. The final remedy at your disposal is to never frequent that restaurant again.

Advice to restaurant staff, if you can't stand the heat, you should get out of the restaurant business.

Chapter Twelve
At Home (Parenting and Family Relations)...

Yelling

When did yelling become the common language of families? Earlier in this book the ineffectiveness of yelling was discussed. Families seem to have a particularly hard time realizing yelling as ineffective. When family members yell at each other it is clear sign that this family has no respect for each other, or they are hard of hearing, but even that is no excuse for the current volume in families. If a family has no respect for itself then all order and structure breaks down and chaos ensues.

If a parent thinks they have to yell at a child to get their point across, they are fundamentally mistaken. The very act of yelling underscores the fact that your child is not listening to you. All the raising of your voice and showing negative emotion will not magically make your child listen to you. Quite the opposite as discussed in an earlier section of the book, just ask yourself what is the first thing you do when someone approaches you angry, yelling, screaming? Most people simply turn-off the screamer and ignore the message. The end result is that the whole point of being so angry and showing so much emotion is lost on the other person. So why do it?

Tipping the COW: Better method of getting through to children is to give firm consequences for not listening. Give consequences that they can and will feel. Make sure they follow the consequences and you follow through on enforcing the consequences. This dynamic between setting consequences that children will feel and enforcing these consequences firmly and consistently is the most important give and take in parenting. It is during this confrontation that the foundation of respect between parent and child is established. If a parent weakens in this confrontation, then the child will not respect the parent.

Question: "Billy, do your parents yell at you?" Answer: "No, but I notice that every other adult talks so softly."

Do the RR technique discussed earlier. The more you (parents) stop modeling yelling as a form of communication, the less it will appear in your household. The RR technique will help you stop the yelling and negative emotions that seem to invade our households so easily.

Setting Consequences

It is important to point out that being a good parent and treating your children civilly means not backing down in this consequence setting confrontation. An earlier chapter discussed not enabling others for their bad behavior. The same rules apply here. If a parent is not consistent and remain steadfast in enforcing the consequences for their child, they are not being a 'good guy' they are being inconsistent and ultimately a 'bad parent'.

The ultimate result of being a parent that is in control and firm with their children is a family at peace and children who feel safe. Attaining this peace is the definition of civil behavior in families. Children respect parents who set clear boundaries and can be counted on because their home life has rules and order. A home with rules and order is predictable. It becomes an island in a world that is often unpredictable and confusing to the child. The home becomes a civil place to live.

We have been discussing how to gain respect as a parent but it is equally important to treat children with respect. One of the building blocks of respecting children is to understand that they are children and they will fail. This sounds like a simple statement, but it is so important and so misunderstood by parents that it deserves more consideration.

Many parents expect children to approach life in the style and with the skills that they as adults possess. The problem is that parents have years of socialization, experience and training at life that children have not gained. But, parents get very disappointed and angry with their children when they haven't done something exactly the way they would do it. This happens constantly between parents and their children. These parents place their needs and expectations before the children's. They are COW parents.

Why don't children do things the way we want them to do them? Because they <u>are</u> children. Age doesn't matter, they are not finished products by definition. Even if a young person is in their early twenties, their life experience cannot approach that of their parents.

Tipping the COW: Parents need to be more patient and to lower their expectations of their children. If they lower their expectations then parents will be less disappointed, less angry and thus more in control of their families. This is the essence of civility, respecting where children are in their development and what they are capable of in their actions. This means that parents need to keep check on their expectations of their children. Keep your expectations low and your goals high.

The nation is alarmed by the youth violence that is sweeping across our country. So much of it appears to have teasing or bullying at its root. What a better indictment for the search for civil behavior than to help prevent this epidemic. If we surround our youth with a world that treats them civilly and demands them to treat others the same way then these episodes would be prevented. Even if youth see others acting without civility, if they have plenty of examples of civil behavior surrounding them there will be a greater chance that they will follow these positive examples.

Children, by definition act uncivilized at times. By definition, sure, think about it. Children are unfinished products; consequently, they will yell, scream, act disrespectful, have tantrums and on and on. And these are not just pre-teens being discussed here. This is also so true when adults are confronting teenagers or youth well into their early twenties. If adults could just remember this golden rule that young people are a work in progress, then adults could better keep control over their children.

Unfortunately, so many parents respond to youth's disrespectful behavior by being disrespectful right back. If their kids are yelling and using foul language, they feel that they have to respond in kind or their children will not obey them. Of course, nothing could be farther from the truth. The more an adult yells and bullies a child, the more the child learns that this is how people are supposed to behave.

Tipping the COW: The best parenting is to take a business-like approach toward children. They will see that you mean business and you will feel more calm and in control. Your attitude should mimic your approach, be business-like in your attitude as well.

Kids and Drugs

For many years the so called experts and the general public had been adapting the totally wrong approach toward preventing young people to use drugs. Instead of taking a civil, respectful approach to keeping young people away from drugs, adult society tried to scare youth into not doing drugs. Unfortunately, no one consulted anyone who knew the personality of kids. Kids love to be rebellious and to do the forbidden. So, the more adults said that drugs were evil, the more young people wanted to do them or just didn't care. So then we tried the message that drugs hurt you, but again, anyone who knows kids knows that they feel invincible. Their attitude toward life is to throw caution to the wind. So, again, the more adults said your going to hurt yourself, the more kids said, "Oh, yea, nothing is going to happen to me. I can handle it." And for the most part, they were right. Then we tried to police them into stopping their drug use. Adults said, "You're going to go to jail." Unfortunately, this message violated a fundamental precept in parenting youth, that is, if you are going to say something you had better be able to back it up and follow through. Every effective parent of a teen or preteen will testify to this principle. Society could not back up the threat of going to jail or even being punished for catching kids with drugs. Most police don't bother with the small amounts of pot they find on kids. When it comes to drinking, the police shockingly consider underage drinking as acceptable behavior of the teenage years.

Tipping the COW: It is absolutely uncivilized behavior of a society to allow such large numbers of its youth to use drugs (Include alcohol here because it is a drug and still the number one drug problem in this country.) How do we not allow our kids to drink and drug? We talk to them, WE CONTROL THEM, model for them, mentor them and we punish (Ooops! Not supposed to say that word, punish, now-a-days.) them for unacceptable behavior. We need to say something to our kids about drugs. Don't let it be an unmentionable secret around your house. We need to say NO and to let them know what strong consequences we will inflict upon them if they use drugs.

Similarly, if you see other kids doing drugs you need to say something to them. It is unacceptable for a group of kids to be drinking and sitting against your garage door late into the night. Shag them away. Call the police. If more people did this, young people will get the message that this is unacceptable.

In early America, there was a system of play mamas and play papas that watched over all the kids in the community. If a young person was about to do something bad, you betcha that some adult voice would ring out from nowhere and tell them to stop. I called this network the Venetian Blinds Brigade. I call it such because in those days, if kids were making noise in the street the window blinds would immediately raise up with that distinctive clatter that resulted from the cord being yanked furiously by an adult needing to look out the window at the raucous.

Youth are COWs by Nature

Youth are COWs by definition. Being a COW while you're young is not a bad thing, it is a developmental thing. Maturation is the process by which a person moves out of COW thinking and COW actions. Children learn coping skills as they give up COWping skills. Until they are young adults, they do not concern themselves with the needs of others. This is a fact of their psychological and cognitive development. Don't expect young people to be other than COWs. Our goal here is to begin to establish patterns in young people that will turn into non-COW habits.

Let's give a clear example of this mechanism. A friend of mine moved into a high-rise building when his boy and girl were quite young. My friend is totally not COW. He holds doors for people, he always has a hello and a smile for others, etc. One day, after years of living in this high-rise, the doorman approached my friend and said, "You have the nicest children, when they are alone, they hold doors open for everybody, they always smile and say hello when they walk through the lobby, and I wish everybody's kids were like yours." This comment made my friend reflect on how this came about. He then realized how his constant behavior and his instruction of them to do this for people developed habits that are now ingrained. These two kids are normal, typical kids, but by modeling and mentoring them in non-COW behavior, they will behave differently than the majority of teens. It is uncivilized not to do this type of modeling and instruction for our young people. When children are small point out civilized behavior, emphasize it, model it and Voila'! They will act civilized as they grow older.

Old adage: 'If it looks like a COW, and acts like a COW, it was probably raised by COWs.'

Prevention Programs

Another uncivilized thing we do to kids is these drug prevention programs in schools. Schools subject the students to a drug curriculum that is typically embedded into some science or health curriculum and take two weeks to try and teach kids not to use drugs or drink. The other mechanism schools use is to hold special presentations and expect that in an hour or two presentation that all the students will change their attitudes toward drugs. It would be better to call these presentations dog-and-pony shows because the kids gain very little from these one-time efforts.

The epitome of these efforts is a program run by the state police departments called, DARE. The police send an officer into the schools to teach the students about drugs and drinking. He or she comes into the school and the classrooms in uniform. Right there the message becomes diluted because of what a uniformed officer represents to most students. No, it's not that the majority of kids have been in trouble with the law or have had a bad personal experience with the police. A police officer represents adult authority and the boundaries that kids want and need to test in their youth so the immediate reaction to this officer is, "Ok, here's what we're <u>supposed</u> to do. He's telling us the rules." There have been many studies that show that the DARE program is ineffective, yet we continue to shove it down the throat of students. Why? Because it makes adults feel like they are doing something about the drug problem in youth. So here all adults are acting like COWs because adults are saying to the youth, we know what you need better than you can tell us so here take this.

Tipping the COW: Prevention should attack the drug problem in the same way that youth are attracted to drugs. A prevention program should surround our youth with a barrage of messages that tell them not to use drugs. Kids don't get involved in drugs by a tiny little experience hidden in some far corner of their existence. They get involved in drugs because it surrounds their existence. Prevention cannot try to be effective without using the same means. Prevention cannot continue to be kept in some isolated little corner of their lives if we want to stop this problem in young people. They must be surrounded by prevention in their world. Just like the messages to do drugs surrounds them daily.

Prevention shouldn't be the assignment of a health or science class for two weeks out of the year. Prevention should be a part of every class, every day. Prevention should ooze out the building at every crack and crevice.

Each teacher and staff member at the school should echo an anti-drug message and an anti-drug lifestyle.

We haven't battled drugs in a civilized way. Like Vietnam, if this is a war, then give us the tools to fight this war. Let's not play around with the politically correct things to do. Let's fight the war, win it, and move onto curing cancer. We need to surround kids in an environment that gives anti-drug messages. This is doable, cost effective but we just don't feel it is that important.

Surrounding young people with civility in the family, at school, and in the community would be the best form of drug prevention. Just as youth are surrounded by the temptation of using drugs, the best remedy is to counter these temptations on the same playing field.

Mental Health Professionals

The mental health field is a big ripe grazing pasture for COWs. Here is a field that utilizes the attitude and personality of the helper as the tools of the trade, yet so many of the practitioners of mental services have the social skills of a dead fish.

A common complaint of people who refer clients to mental health professionals is that they call them and the professional doesn't return the call or at best calls back days later. More puzzling is the mental health provider who is treating a young person and a parent calls with some questions and the provider hides under the veil of 'confidentiality' so they can't answer the simplest, most general question. They do this even though the parent is paying the bill for the services. Do you know any other service provider that can get away with this? Yet, people do put up with this type of service. No wonder mental health services receive little respect in the public's eye. Mental health care is trying to get equal payment with other health care services by legislative action, but unless mental health providers garner more respect in the public's eye, this parity will have little success.

Why do mental health providers receive so little respect? The reasons are clear:

> ➢ They lack common sense customer service techniques.
> ➢ Too many are poorly trained.
> ➢ Too many are poorly supervised.
> ➢ They are uncommunicative or simply can't communicate with people.
> ➢ They are too unregulated at the lower levels.
> ➢ There are too many spurious practices: examples: re-birthing, primal therapy, coaches, tantra therapists, and on and on.
> ➢ Addiction therapists who become qualified simply because they have suffered the addiction.
> ➢ Too many have problems of their own that overwhelm them and keep them from helping others.
> ➢ Too many enter this field for the wrong reasons.
> ➢ Too many are out of touch with the culture and society that their clients live in.

Mental health care is a wonderful profession, one of the most noble in all of health care when delivered by a well-trained, socially skilled and compassionate provider. It is a field that has a strong science to bolster its techniques and it works wonders in helping to ease the suffering of others, but it must go on a crusade to rid itself of these charlatan practitioners and inadequate practitioners who hang around the fringes of this profession and get associated with the rest of the profession.

Tipping the COW: If you go to a therapist and they do not treat you in a social, compassionate manner, leave. Don't stand for any behavior that you wouldn't tolerate in any other service you are purchasing. If you don't feel comfortable with the personality of the provider, then run for the hills and don't look back. Including, don't stand for the lack of results and definitive statements in your mental health care. There are so many rich and successful techniques that mental health can share with you, yet the public's entrance into this marvelous field is so often clouded by these fringe players.

Chapter Thirteen
Turn in your own COWs

This book is a start. It is not meant to be an exhaustive list of all the uncivilized behavior we all suffer through each day. Please send your own COWs into the publisher. Call, email, or snail mail them to the addresses given inside this book. Or call 1-866-DRMAYER. You will find that sending in a COW is a very therapeutic way to cope with these injustices. And give any COW you know or experience a copy of this book. This is a great way to anonymously let the COW know how their behavior affects others. Maybe we can change COWs if they all are confronted with their actions. Put a bookmark in the section that describes their COW-like behavior. The book will make a wonderful holiday gift item as well.

Remember when you turn in your COWs to add your method of *Tipping the COW*. The best of these submissions will be included in the next edition of this book. Each accepted submission will be entered into a contest to receive a golden COW as a trophy of your civilized behavior.

Have fun tipping over the COWs of the World!

The End

About the Author

Dr. John E. Mayer is a practicing clinical psychologist. He has been helping people change their lives for over 25 years. He is a nationally known clinician, author, lecturer, and consultant. Dr. Mayer has authored 11 books, including: <u>The 3 Week Family Fat Cure</u>, Shadow Warrior (a novel), books on Drug, smoking and gang prevention and athletic coaching. Dr. Mayer received his doctorate from Northwestern Univ. Medical School. He is a diplomate in both clinical and sports psychology. The highest status one can attain in each of these fields, an exceptional accomplishment in <u>two</u> fields. Dr. Mayer is married and has two wonderful children.

Printed in the United Kingdom
by Lightning Source UK Ltd.
102412UKS00002B/251